The
Whisky
Barons

The Whisky Barons

ALLEN ANDREWS

THE CLASSIC
EXPRESSIONS | ANGELS' SHARE

The Angels' Share is an imprint of
Neil Wilson Publishing Ltd
303a The Pentagon Centre
36 Washington Street
Glasgow
G3 8AZ

Tel: 0141 221 1117
Fax: 0141 221 5363
E-mail: info@nwp.sol.co.uk
www.angelshare.co.uk

First published in 1977 by
Jupiter Books (London) Limited.
This edition published in 2002 by
The Angels' Share.

A catalogue record for this book is
available from the British Library.
ISBN 1-897784-84-8

Printed in Finland by WS Bookwell
Design by Belstane

Contents

Publisher's Note

I FIRST came across Allen Andrew's *The Whisky Barons* when I was about to write my first whisky book in the early eighties. I was trawling the catalogues of antiquarian booksellers in the hope that I could source many of the research titles I required.

Twenty years on, I am still driven by that somewhat selfish motive to track down these rare books. But as I have gradually turned into a full-time publisher I have been moved to look at many of these volumes in a different light. In 1987, when I was involved in Lochar Publishing, I took my first step into re-issuing a classic whisky text. In partnership with Mainstream Publishing of Edinburgh, we re-published Alfred Barnard's *The Whisky Distilleries of the United Kingdom* a century after its first edition. The printing quickly sold out and although we did not reprint, in 2000 a new edition emerged from Rasch*edition* Osnabrück in Germany and is still available.

There are many rare whisky volumes gathering dust that deserve a similar new lease of life. *The Whisky Barons* is one such and I toyed with the idea of re-issuing it for several years. I was frustrated in that I could neither trace Allen Andrews nor Jupiter Books of London who first published the volume in 1977. Andrews was born in 1913 and died in 1984 in London but I simply could find no record of him. I tried the Publisher's Association, the Society of Authors and contacts in the whisky trade to no avail. Nor could I find any trace of him from Zimmerman's liquor store in Chicago, where he had sourced much of his Scotch. The Internet only brought confusing messages and so I decided to publish his work in 2002 and hope that someone in his family would contact me.

The Whisky Barons is therefore the first of many books on whisky that I hope to re-issue in a series called The Classic Expressions. These will cover the broadest spectrum of previously published material and will include the more technical works as well as the more romantic and idiosyncratic titles.

At the very least I hope that this will make the search for these scarce volumes far less frustrating than it has been for me over the past two decades.

Neil Wilson, Glasgow, 2002

SCOTCH WHISKY is a subject which tends to bring out in writers a fey quality which they manfully repress from their other work. I am therefore indebted to the factual records of the principal archivist of the complex growth and involutions of the trade, Ross Wilson, and in particular to his books, *Scotch: The Formative Years* (London, Constable, 1970) and *Scotch Made Easy* (London, Hutchinson, 1959).

Professor David Daiches has written an extremely authoritative record which is gracefully lightened by his own unintimidated and informative personal critique on named blends and single malts: a university professor who works with seven different single malts on his desk is surely a living challenge to the old canard that entire pot-still whisky is unsuitable for people in sedentary occupations. The book is: *Scotch Whisky: Its Past and Present* (London, Deutsch, 1969 and Birlinn, Edinburgh, 1995).

An amateur's history, with recollections of the author's youth spent at Balmenach Distillery speckling a comprehensive survey, is: Sir Robert Bruce Lockhart, *Scotch: The Whisky of Scotland in Fact and Story* (London, Putnam, 1951 and 1959 and NWP, Glasgow, 1995).

I have consulted some 500 autobiographies and memoirs relating to the period, but find a lamentable lack of contemporary appreciation of the giants who were striding out of puberty at the end of the nineteenth century, and I must be restricted to the recommendation, if only for the pictures by Sidney Cowell, who was illustrating *Sherlock Holmes* at about that time of TR Dewar's *A Ramble Round the Globe* with 220 illustrations (London, Chatto & Windus, 1904).

For information on the status of various Scotch whiskies in the American market, I am indebted to Max Zimmerman, of Zimmerman's, 240 West Randolph Street, Chicago, friend and supplier over fifteen years to myself and Captain J Wilson Cook.

A.A.

From Wambling and Wirtching – Whisky Deliver Us!

SCOTCH WHISKY came into the world as a lion from the north, impelled by the whip-cracks of a remarkable set of Scottish impresario ringmasters. Some of them were supremely skilful (and lucky) in mastering every facet of exploitation, including finance. Where a Barnum needed his Bailey, extroverts were supported and advised by shrewd chancellors and administrators. All of them, as the last of the merchant adventurers in individualistic capitalism, showed far more bounce and daring than is considered decent today, and went out with a grand unwhimpering bang as they handed over to Corporation Man. Such were the Whisky Barons, who flourished in the half-century stretching from the Strauss Waltz to the Charleston Age, casually taking advantage of two American disasters which marked either end of the period. The first was the American louse or aphid which brought the vine disease phylloxera to Europe, and virtually extinguished brandy production by the 1880s; the second was the American genius for masochistic misanthropy which permitted the introduction of Prohibition in the 1920s and beyond. Both scourges were

1

highly advantageous to Scotch whisky. But battles are not won only through weakness in the enemy line; generals are needed with the wit to perceive and exploit opportunities.

This was an attribute of the only Englishman who is celebrated here – Francis Berry, who in his time was neither lionised nor baronised. The rest moved up in the Honours List, rarely quitting under the rank of baronet, as witness the two (White Label) Dewars, John Baron Forteviot and Thomas Baron Dewar; James (Black and White) Buchanan, Baron Woolavington; James (Johnnie Walker) Baron Stevenson and Sir Alexander Walker, KBE; Sir Peter (White Horse) Mackie, Baronet; and Earl Haig, Viscount Dawick, Baron Haig and Laird of Bemersyde, who won his honours in World War I but used them to adorn John Haig and the Distillers Company.

By a curious irony, every one of the honours awarded to the Whisky Barons (except the Dewars' first steps on the ladder and Stevenson's last) was bestowed by the king on the advice of the most cunning and ferocious Prohibitionist of all. This was Prime Minister David Lloyd George, self-appointed scourge of what he called (employing his own capitals) the Drink Trade. Occasionally he varied this term of reproach to the phrase Liquor Traffic, which put it in his eyes on about the same level as the White Slave Traffic. The extraordinary feature about Lloyd George's theatrical abhorrence of liquor was that, hating the Drink Trade as he did, he was compelled to win the war – in such measure as it was won – by the employment of Haig (of John Haig) as his commander-in-chief and Stevenson (of Johnnie Walker) as his backroom overlord of munitions.

The other interesting commentary is that, having put the

Liquor Traffic and the White Slave Traffic on roughly the same footing, Lloyd George did not in his private life abstain from having a bit on the side, whether it was a social glass of stimulant or a white slave. But, to do him justice, he did prefer women to whisky. His appetite was, in fact, voracious, but in his conventionality he did not marry his mistress of thirty years' standing until after the death of his wife. Neither wife nor mistress, however, barred him from making passes at anyone handy, as a tipsy man will slide along a bar up-ending other people's unfinished glasses. Lloyd George took very seriously his power of patronage through the Honours List (and additionally raked in a considerable augmentation of his political funds, which perhaps promoted him into the Honours Traffic). The secretary whom he put in charge of honours applications and suggestions realized that there were other suggestions in the offing as well. She found the Prime Minister 'a bit amorous', which, she has since confided to the author, 'I didn't like at all – I was very pure then. Perhaps, if I'd used my loaf, I'd have ended up with more than an OBE.'

Before the era of the Whisky Barons, the Scots had for many centuries maintained a remarkable secrecy about their whisky, which they had been distilling from malted and unmalted barley for a thousand years as *uisge beatha*, one of the Gaelic names for 'water of life', the first word of which is now rendered as 'whisky'. About once in every hundred years some English scholar would discover and record the wonderful properties of this rare drink, but without making a lasting impact on the south. The most fulsome in his praises was Raphael Holinshed, who in his *Chronicles of England, Scotland and Ireland* printed in 1577 declared that whisky, taken in moderation, cut phlegm, dispelled melancholia, cured dropsy and strangury (a condition of slow and painful urination), reduced the stone and expelled gravel, and subdued wind with its accompanying inconveniences of a wambling stomach and a wirtching belly.

Holinshed's full list of the powers of whisky is worth reprinting as a public notice suitable for any bar or homoeopathic doctor's waiting-room:

Beying moderatelie taken, it sloweth age; it strengtheneth youthe; it helpeth digestion; it cutteth fleume; it abandoneth melancholic; it relisheth the harte; it lighteneth the mynde; it quickeneth the spirites; it cureth the hydropsie; it healeth the strangury; it pounceth the stone; it repelleth gravel; it puffeth away ventositie; it kepyth and preserveth the head from whyrling – the eyes from dazelyng – the tongue from lispyng – the mouth from snafflyng [speaking through the nose] – the teeth from chatteryng – the throte from ratlyng the weasan [windpipe] from stieflyng – the stomach from wamblyng – the harte from swellyng – the bellie from wirtchyng – the guts from rumblyng – the hands from shiueryng – the sinowes from shrinkyng – the veynes from crumplyng – the bones from soakyng ... Truly it is a souueraine liquor.

No such eloquent and embracing exposition of the medicinal powers of whisky was compiled again until 1921, when the citizens of the United States found that the only way to get a drop of Scotch with legality was to recognize the old wambling and wirtching, revive the old lore of the curative powers of whisky, and go out smartly to obtain a doctor's prescription for it. Consequently whisky began to be consumed in medicine glasses and, through faith, for medicinal purposes at the rate of about twenty-seven million gallons a year. As the *Saturday Evening Post* wryly commented, 'A nation that has developed enough sickness in eight months to require 18 million gallons of whisky to alleviate its suffering may be depended on to remain sick indefinitely.'

Fortunately for everyone, the sickness did not prove terminal. The Whisky Barons had never set up as pharmaceutical chemists, and the role did not chime with the remarkable honesty which, in general, they combined with their enthusiasm as salesmen. Tommy Dewar, it was true, had been confronted by a similar situation thirty years before. When travelling across a Prohibition state in North America, he had gone, as recommended, to a drug store. The owner sold him a capacious bottle of Cholera Mixture which, on the other side, bore Dewar's own label as his standard blend. He took it unquestioningly, and never caught cholera afterwards.

James Buchanan
Courtesy of Diageo Archive

CHAPTER TWO

'I marvel at my supreme self-confidence!'

THERE WAS A MUSIC-HALL SONG well known to James Buchanan, and he hummed it to himself as he eased his admirably slim hips into a pair of immaculately cut trousers which, once adjusted, seemed to stand up by themselves, quite creaseless, and waft him forward to success.

> *How did you get your trousers on?*
> *And did they hurt you much?*

sang Buchanan in mocking self-satisfaction as he smoothed down the exquisite fall of his frock coat, checked the fastenings of his discreet personal jewellery, flashed his silk hat in a shining arc, and set off for the Mansion House.

Jimmy Buchanan shone like the sun in a City of London which, except on the brightest days, was a far gloomier place in the 1880s than it is today. There were no tall buildings, but that fact only brought the chimney smoke nearer the ground. The fog, though not always of the density of a London Particular, was a far more constant feature, so that the free-floating dome of St Paul's often gleamed, as if quite detached from the world of business, in a sun that rarely reached the streets that fell down towards the Thames.

Lord Woolavington with his daughter at Mannock Moors
Radio Times/Hulton

There were no fumes from internal combustion engines, but far deadlier eruptions of smoke and soot poured forth in spreading clouds from the strategic vents and stations of the coal-burning Metropolitan Railway. From these station exits there staggered a mob of smutty gentlemen coughing their hearts out as they breathed in their only substitute for fresh air. The Inner Circle had just been completed, first by an extension west from Aldgate, then by the opening of the line from Westminster to Mansion House. But mechanical breakdowns, and a lack of communication between officials and passengers, produced a frustration which modern passengers may perhaps find some comfort in recognizing. A friend of Buchanan's, baulked from keeping an appointment with him, passed his time by composing this questionnaire:

As we have already waited three-quarters of an hour in the centre of a dark and stuffy tunnel, and I am due in the City

*half an hour ago, perhaps it would be as well to inquire if
there is a stoppage on the line.*

*Guard, have you any reason to suppose that the train has
been stopped in order to allow the engine-driver and stoker
to have a quiet game of cribbage behind the coals in the
tender?*

*As I have been particularly recommended by my doctor to
'select a bracing air,' and as I suffer from asthma and chronic
bronchitis, I really don't think that this detention in a
sulphurous sewer near Baker Street for a whole hour is likely
to improve my general health. Porter, is my bed made up in
the wagon-lit which now runs between Earls Court and the
Mansion House?*

An alternative method of getting around was to take the
horsedrawn omnibus. This was despised by the newly rich – of
whom in this brash age of the fast buck there were a considerable
number – but accepted by the aristocracy. Buchanan cherished a
joke going the rounds centering on a conversation between a
nouveau riche and a well-born lady: 'Society's getting much too
mixed, yer ladyship. I can assure you, when Lady M's a-drivin'
about London in one of 'er hopen carriages, she 'ardly dares look
up, for fear o' seein' someone she knows on the top of a
homnibus.' To which the blueblooded maiden replied: 'Yes, very
sad. She'll often see Papa there, but never me. Mamma and I
always go inside.' The inevitable accompaniment of massive
horse-drawn traffic was the health hazard and inconvenience of
the constant droppings, fly-crowned in the heat and liquid
sewage in the rain; and ragged crossing-sweepers were still an

important sector of the city personnel, to sweep a clean path for bright boots and trailing skirts.

James Buchanan was a man of delicate health, who in theory should never have strayed far from the fresh glens of his home ground, the tree-clad Trossachs and the lochs of Lomond and Katrine. Nevertheless, he made his decision to go to London – and his instinct seems to have been right, as he lived to the age of eighty-six. Once in the metropolis, he lived in a brave conception of metropolitan style, and cut an unforgettably fine figure.

He was very tall and slim, lantern-jawed and red-haired with strong eyebrows and a broad shelf of an auburn moustache. His high silk hat crowned an ensemble of elegant suiting with an orchid in the buttonhole of his frock-coat, and a pearl pin below the huge tie-knot of the deep starched collar which he carried gracefully round his long neck. In this great style he travelled round London – but not in hansom cab or growler, omnibus or Underground train. He drove an outstandingly smart two-wheeled buggy, brightly painted with shining red wheels. And whenever he jumped down he cast the reins to his 'tiger', an elegantly liveried young groom who normally sat behind him during his regal progress. Buchanan was a man to be seen, noted and admired. It was a very necessary image for a Scotsman whose mission it was to sell, first to London and then to the world, this novel potion, Scotch whisky. Blended Scotch whisky. Buchanan's blend. A product which in a very short time had, in proprietary self-defence, to be registered as The Buchanan Blend.

Of all the Whisky Barons, Buchanan was for long the most individualistic, solitary in business if not in his social pleasures. He was born in August 1849 in Brockville, Ontario, the youngest son of Scottish emigrants who speedily recrossed the Atlantic. Because of his delicate health he was educated privately. He had family connections in the middle ranks of commerce, and at the age of fourteen went to Glasgow to work in the office of a shipping firm in which a cousin was a partner. After three years he became a Customs House clearing clerk at £20 a year. The salary was never increased, and at the end of his contract Buchanan ruefully realized that in six years he had only doubled the earnings he had been offered when he left school. He joined his brother, who was a grain merchant in Glasgow, and thus became at least indirectly connected with the cereals that were being distilled for whisky. For an ambitious man, Buchanan displayed remarkable patience, and it was only after a further ten years that, at the age of thirty, he capitulated to the vision of what Dr Johnson called 'the noblest prospect which a Scotchman ever sees, the high road that leads him to England'. Buchanan came to London to act as agent for Charles Mackinlay & Company, the whisky merchants.

He was an innocent abroad. 'I was handicapped very much at the beginning by being an entire stranger,' he later recalled. 'I only knew two friends in the whole City of London, and they were of no assistance to me in my start in business, although they were staunch and kind. However, I was determined to make a success of my life, and that I should fail to do so never entered my head.'

Buchanan therefore bided his time. This outstanding capacity for a painstaking 'casing of the joint' contrasts indelibly with the speed of his pounce when he struck. He was certainly not accumulating capital during this period, for he had to borrow to the hilt when the time came. But he was acquiring experience.

After five years he was ready. He returned to Leith, seeking a partnership in a whisky trader's, but was rejected. He decided to set up in London on his own account. He went to WP Lowrie, chairman of a Glasgow firm which owned malt distilleries but which had also gone very early into the business of blending whisky. Lowrie not only lent him the capital to set himself up, but guaranteed the supplies of whisky which he needed. So Buchanan came south again and established himself as the sole proprietor of James Buchanan & Company, of the City of London (but with an accommodation address in Glasgow), producers of The Buchanan Blend of Fine Old Scotch Whiskies.

His timing was impeccable. This was the breakthrough point for blended Scotch whisky. And this large, lithe red-haired Scot seemed likely to be the vanguard of the breakthrough as he drove his beautiful black pony in the smartest equipage in the City, and gathered the appreciative glances then which are now reserved for sports cars. Buchanan was no vapid dandy. He was

The WP Lowrie workforce, Washington Street, Glasgow, c.1900
Courtesy of Diageo Archive

The WP Lowrie yard, Glasgow, c.1900
Courtesy of Diageo Archive

a shrewd man of thirty-five who had possibly been a late developer in business enterprise, but once racing he had the guts to sprint and the personality to charm, right from the start. Blended Scotch whisky had to move. The Buchanan Blend, made up in casks in Glasgow, was moved in casks to London and moved swiftly out in casks to the bars of the metropolis. That was the way whisky was sold in those days, and Buchanan was selling it well. Within a year of setting up in the city he had repaid Lowrie the original loan made to start the business and, renewing his independence, confirmed his previous contracts with Lowrie for supplies. But it was Buchanan, now clearly paying the piper, who called the tune. He did not light upon The Buchanan Blend engraved on tablets on the summit of Ben A'an above his native Loch Katrine, nor was the formula brought to him one night in a deep dream of peace by courtesy of Abou Ben

Adhem. In London he could only talk, talk, talk and test, test, test as he discussed his blend with customers. He was not always driving his buggy. There was often, in the early days, need of the then spartan train trip to Glasgow to adjust the blend according to the taste he was discovering. Jimmy Buchanan was in the eye of a hurricane, manipulating a revolution which he had not incited. All that concerned him was that he should emerge in one piece and an acknowledged victor.

Circumstances favoured a radical change in the drinking habits of the English. But Buchanan was cast in the mould of the Bernard Shaw character who said, 'I don't believe in circumstances. The people who get on in this world are the people who get up and look for the circumstances they want.'

Why were the 1880s the critical period for the acceptance of Scotch whisky? The principal spirits drunk in the south had been brandy and gin, with rum a steady ingredient for toddy. Gin had been for two centuries a low-class drink, ever since King William III had introduced it from Holland, and had slapped high taxes on its rival brandy once the London distillers had mastered the manufacture. In its worst form, gin was never more esoteric than a highly distilled, tasteless alcohol, unimproved by maturing, flavoured with juniper and enlivened with sulphuric acid and oil of turpentine to add kick as well as taste. But it was offered at middle-class tables in the 1880s in its refined form as imported 'hollands', and in those circles it was still reputed as socially superior to whisky, though well below brandy.

Brandy was served not only as a liqueur, but as a weaker daytime beverage (like whisky and water today) in the form of brandy and soda, generally called 'B and S'. But brandy had fallen on evil times. True brandy can only be the distillation of wine made from grapes. If the grapes fail, the source is killed. In the third quarter of the nineteenth century there had been a succession of disasters. First, a mildew called oidium devastated the vineyards and crippled the production of wine. When, after twenty years, a partial cure for this pestilence had been developed, there was an even more destructive invasion from America of an aphid called phylloxera, a yellow louse related to the greenfly family of insects. This almost halved French wine production and was overcome eventually only by tearing out all the vines and replacing them with stocks known to be immune to the pest. But another form of mildew then attacked the vines.

In the meantime, brandy production was very seriously diminished. The effect was cumulative, since the best brandy is matured in cask over twenty years, but the impact on prices was immediate. As a result, not only was brandy much scarcer in England, but also much more expensive, and what brandy was offered, in the 'B and S' for example, was often suspect. In the mid-eighties some gentlemen's club butlers were said to be successfully offering sherry for brandy, and a satirical advertisement for a bookmaker ('Find me at the same old spot – bottom of horsepond') promised 'Cigarettes and brandy, both British, for all British backers'.

Whisky was well enough known, but always as something of a joke. It was what you got when you went to Scotland – and the upper classes, of course, did go to Scotland for deer-stalking, for fishing and for shooting in a far more regular pattern than nowadays. Whisky was reputed to be an open-air drink, which you could just about master before it mastered you by the stream or on the moor – though even then the prospects were dubious. (Topical joke: the Laird's brother-in-law to the keeper, 'Very strange, Lachlan. I'm having no luck, yet I seem to see two birds in place of one. That was surely very strong whiskey [the current spelling] your master gave me at lunch!' Keeper: 'Maybe aye and maybe no. The whuskey was goot. But any way ye dinna manage to hit the right bird o' the twa!')

Scotland itself, always a bit of a joke to the southerners, was going through a particularly bad period as far as its image was concerned. Sir Walter Scott had romanticized the country for the Scottish. Prince Albert, of all people, had romanticized it for the courtiers, with his ludicrous likening of Balmoral to Saxe-Coburg-Gotha [a central European dukedom which was admittedly only slightly bigger in area than the Balmoral estate] and his even more ludicrous insistence on the kilt – a spurious Highland dress which he forced on his son and heir the Prince of Wales, afterwards King Edward VII, even to be worn in Paris at the Court of the Emperor of the French. The landed aristocracy had no need to romanticize Scotland. Either they owned most of it, and steadily depopulated it in favour of stags, or they had a cousin who owned a large slice of it and could give them the use of stream, moor or glen whenever the sporting instinct raised its liquidating head. The new people from England who had suddenly fallen into ecstasy over Scotland were the prosperous middle class, who were running at their usual distance of about one generation behind the Royal Family. They spurted to become tourists in North Britain and, like many tourists, quarrelled with their hosts immediately as soon as they were offered food which differed in any respect from the fodder served at home. *The Times* printed a spate of letters condemning the 'McAutocrats of the Breakfast Table' and among other reactions the following warning notice was printed:

ADVICE TO TOURISTS. – Where to go in Scotland. 'Bock agen.' If you're a party, and can be independent of arbitrary Hotel rules, travel as COOK'S Tourists, and take the Tourist's Cook with you. Certainly the Scotch Hotel-Keeper for discourtesy, incivility, and unaccommodativeness ought, in the Land of Cakes, to 'take the cake' and eat it himself.

The episcopalian English tourist, in fact, found himself in unexpected alliance with the ministers of the Scots Kirk – but only because, in the main, they were all against the whisky. It was not the best atmosphere in which to cultivate the sale in London of a new tipple from the north.

Buchanan, as a salesman, perceived the two most glaring disadvantages of Scotch whisky, which Londoners were not analytical enough to formulate: that they were often not sure what they were going to get; and when they got it they did not like it. Buchanan could enunciate this in 1885, perhaps more clearly than could be done now, even though the Scotch whisky provided for the south then was mainly the single malt whisky which is held in such high reverence today.

That is to say, the Scotch whisky generally offered in London, tapped straight into the glass from a cask at the bar, was a 'single malt' which had been (1) wholly distilled from the product of malted barley which had been allowed to germinate to a point where it could turn its starch into sugar, and had then been (2) dried over peat fires, and (3) mixed with 'special', ie, local spring, water before fermentation into alcohol, and (4) distilled in a manner by which it carried over into the vapour traces of the peat-tinged barleycorn oil which give malt whisky its flavour.

It was Buchanan's insight that convinced him that the English public – and later the world public – did not like the full flavour of Scotch malt whisky, but preferred something more bland. He made this judgement in simplicity, as a man who was seeking a product he could sell. It was easier for him to reach this decision than it would have been for his successors, because he was not concerned with the heresy involved. Nowadays there is a holy awe built up around malt whisky which makes it in theory a sacred untouchable. Malt whisky has a magic connotation, and its image must not be defiled. It is still the fact that not many people drink it entire, and that if the public taste did change to all-malt whisky there would not be enough to go round.

Most Scotch whisky drunk today consists of malt blended with grain whiskies. Grain whiskies are not principally produced from malted barley, but from other cereals whose starch is converted by enzymes from a little additional malted barley. The cereal has *not* been subjected to peat drying. The whisky does *not* depend on the special properties of any local water. It is *not* produced from the traditional pot still, but is distilled in a continuous process in enormous quantity compared with the, say, 2,000 gallons which are made in one operation in the pot still. The unique qualities of malt, peat, local water and pronounced flavour are therefore missing from grain, or 'patent-still' whisky. But it does have taste, it does mature in cask, and it does marry with malt whiskies in blends – differing according to the number of whiskies used (which may be up to forty) and even according to the order in which they are introduced – which have separate identitities as discernible to the expert as fingerprints are to the police.

Buchanan was not the pioneer of blending whisky. There was a young man named Tommy Dewar, busy at that moment packing his bags in Perth before emigrating to London, who on behalf of his family would have vigorously contested any such claim – and Alexander Walker would have reminded both that he had been exporting blended whisky for nearly a generation. Buchanan, however, gave a purposeful rocket-thrust of propaganda to the innovation. He *believed* in the virtues of blended whisky with such infectious enthusiasm. If brandy was to yield in popularity to whisky, Buchanan saw that he still had to combat the market rivals of Irish whiskey and Scottish malt. Both were pot-still whiskies. Pot-still whiskies – if only because of their striking individuality and the comparatively small output of any one pot-distillery – were rare in themselves and therefore unreliable as standard products. A customer could not be sure that he would rhapsodize over the next glass he ordered. The malt distillers began to attack this problem by selling vatted whisky – blends of malt whisky at different stages of maturity and age, but all pot-stilled. Buchanan nailed his standard to his original beliefs that the English did not want pure malt because of its flavour and lack of standardization. He carefully assessed what he thought was a suitable standard Buchanan Blend, and fired full broadsides to call public attention to it.

'What I made up my mind to do,' he recalled in later years, 'was to find a blend sufficiently light and old to please the palate of the user. This I fortunately was able to do, and I made rapid headway ... When I think sometimes I marvel at the supreme self-confidence that upheld me – a young man without capital and with practically no knowledge of the business I was embarking in; a stranger, too, amongst strangers in the City of London. The extraordinary thing is that the possibility of failure never once occurred to me. I had it always before me in my mind that sooner or later I was bound to make a success.

'I need hardly say', he added, 'that I was on the quest for business night and day, getting introductions and getting to know people wherever I could.' Anyone who knew Buchanan would have agreed that it was quite unnecessary for him to say so. As a determined man, past his first youth, resolved to make his fortune, he could have sparked many an unpleasant impact had it not been for the gaiety and vivacity which redressed the balance of his volcanic salesmanship. Sir James Barrie, a Scot himself, declared, 'There are few more impressive sights in the world than a Scotsman on the make.' Buchanan justified ever word of the appraisal. He was a hard grafter, in the English sense of the word, but not without overtones of the American gloss. 'I had to scheme', he admitted, 'to gain accounts that were otherwise difficult.

'One instance ... I had tried repeatedly to open an account with the Associated Music Halls Companies in London, which were then controlled by a well-known figure – Mr Newsom Smith – the head of a large accountancy house and Chairman of the United Music Halls Company. This company comprised practically all the leading music halls of London at the time – the Pavilion, Metropolitan, Oxford, Canterbury and several others.

I could see that it was a very fine opportunity to get a good advertisement for my whisky if I could get the account. It occurred to me one day that if I could manage to get Mr Newsom Smith to audit my accounts and prepare my yearly balance, that I would in this way get in touch with the music halls. Without any delay, I called and saw him, and asked if he would take in hand the audit of my books and accounts. He expressed his pleasure and thanked me for the suggestion. I allowed some little time to elapse before calling to see him again, when I told him I would be very pleased to send in samples and that I hoped to merit a share of his trade. He at once replied that he would be very pleased to send for me the next time they were in the market. I need hardly say that I brought off the business that I desired, and very soon my whisky was the dominant blend in all those London music halls.'

The little square advertisements above the running-order bills of stars like Marie Lloyd and George Robey, reminding patrons that Buchanan's Blend was gushing in the bars, are familiar to ardent theatre-programme collectors. The music hall at that time, resisting the usual attacks on it for its vulgarity, was unexpectedly rescued through the diversion caused by a frontal assault on the Royal Academy – for indecency. A reformer veiling herself as British Matron – they always existed, but it was left to the television era to persuade them to exchange pseudonyms for publicity – led a campaign against the pictures of nudes in the Summer Exhibition. She was supported by a Royal Academician, who had some power as treasurer of the Royal Academy and proposed that henceforth all models at art schools should be clothed. At least it saved sixpence a sitting on the models' fees at the Royal Academy Schools at Burlington House, but the economy did not appeal to Buchanan, in spite of the fact that 'Bang goes saxpence' was already a catchphrase. He kept out of the controversy, however, beyond observing that Horsley's only well-known picture to date, after painting a fresco forty years previously for the House of Lords called *The Spirit of Religion*, bore the title *Caught Napping*, and he remarked that the academician would be hampered in his current task of travelling the country in search of pictures for the Winter Loan Exhibition of Old Masters, by the shock of realizing that all the trees were stripped. *Nuda est veritas et praevalebit*, was his conclusion.

Buchanan called himself a schemer. But there was a Dickensian warmth, as well as perception, behind his most calculated actions. (He was, incidentally, a patron of the Dickens Fellowship, and in his prosperity he named the horse which eventually won the Derby for him Captain Cuttle.) In his later years he seemed to try to cast an aura of sophisticated cupidity around impulses which did not need to be defended against accusations of *naïveté*, only of heart – and hope for the best. As witness his recollections:

One of the most prominent men in the licensed trade, and the owner of a number of very important licensed houses, whom I was very anxious to capture as a customer, proved difficult. He was extraordinarily conservative, and would not make any change in his buying. I called on him regularly for about eighteen months, and he was always perfectly kind and nice to me, but no business resulted.

I found out that he was a widower with two very charming daughters. One of them took charge of his principal licensed house in London – a very nice, intelligent girl, and the younger one had just returned from a convent school in Belgium.

I made myself, of course, as agreeable as possible to the elder girl, and when I called to see her father it occurred to me that one day I would invite her to one of our Burns Club Cinderella Dances which I used to attend, and she said she and her sister would be delighted to come, and they got permission from their father.

In those days the dances were held at Willis's Rooms. I introduced the two young ladies to several of my bachelor friends and told them to be sure and give them every dance. The young ladies enjoyed themselves thoroughly and I saw them off.

The following week when I called to see their father on business as usual, he immediately beckoned me into his office and told me he would never forget my kindness to his two girls, and told me of the loss of his wife, and how much he felt the loss of her in looking after his daughters. The long and the short of it was that I then got the whole of his trade, and every Christmas morning for many years I used to go over and see him at his private house and have a glass of champagne with him and the girls. The outcome was that I got an order for five thousand gallons of scotch whisky.

Inescapably, there seems more artifice in Buchanan's relation of the story, when he was over eighty, to emphasize the craft of getting business, than in what can be deduced from his actions at the time. He was a spontaneous man, brimful of fun, a fellow for a lark. A story told of his genius for promotion, possibly apocryphal but none the less characteristic, concerns his introduction of Buchanan's Blend into a major London hotel that had so far declined to take it. Jimmy Buchanan hired twelve handsome unemployed actors to join him in a grand dinner which had been specially ordered. They arrived in style, in full evening dress, the cynosure of neighbouring eyes. They sat down at table, and the wine waiter approached. 'What will you start with, sir?'

'Buchanan Blend,' said the gorgeous young man who had been placed at the head of the table. An embarrassed pause ensued.

'I'm sorry, we don't have that, sir.'

'What! No Buchanan?' screamed the company in well-drilled horror. 'We can't dine here.' And they swept out, opera cloaks and all, under the fascinated, even sanctifying, gaze of their former fellow-diners.

But Buchanan knew how to employ patience as well as bravado:

A very influential man in our trade – the owner of a large hotel and a number of important retail houses – I found very difficult to capture, but I ultimately did so. He told me one day, 'I have known you now for the last three or four months' (as a matter of fact, I used to dine at his hotel every night) 'and you have never asked me for an order – you are an extraordinary man.' 'Well,' I said, 'the fact is, you are such an important man in the trade and your business is so extensive, that I wanted you to know me a little better than merely as a supper acquaintance before asking you to give me the opportunity of supplying you.' He said, 'I would like you to send me a hogshead of your whisky to try in our café bars.' I told his manager (whom by this time I knew very well) to be sure and run the whisky well when it came. The young ladies behind the bars were also well posted. The whisky was put on tap, and everyone was told about it, and there was a tremendous run on my blend. My friend came to me afterwards and said, 'Well, I have always had a certain "self" [unblended malt] whisky on supply here, but yours I like much better. When I take a little more of the other whisky than usual, the next day I feel good for nothing, but your whisky seems so much pleasanter and lighter. I should like to place an order with you, but I have such a large stock of whisky [naming two very prominent distilleries] that I cannot make room for yours." At this time there was a considerable demand for whisky in the market in Scotland, and I told him I would take samples of the whisky he had in stock and try and dispose of it for him. I recollect the price was six shillings per gallon, and I put an extra sixpence on the price, and by return of post I had sold the whisky, and the difference between the price and the price realized amounted to £175 to my friend's advantage, so my labours were quite appreciated. This was another very large account I was able to open by exercising a little tact.

The footnotes to this anecdote are endless. Buchanan was already a crony of the bar manager. He could influence the barmaids. – By what persuasion? The whisky was 'run well when it came' – meaning that bumper measures were dispensed, an admirable practice before the tyranny of six-out optics, but who paid? Buchanan would never impose such a loss on his patron. 'Everyone was told about it, and there was a tremendous run on my blends'. – How much word-of-mouth and printed publicity went into ensuring that everyone knew about it? 'Your whisky seems so much pleasanter and lighter' – an authentic, otherwise useless, jab at malt whisky, which had long lost the battle by the time Buchanan was reminiscing. Finally, the disposal of 7,000 gallons of malt at eight per cent over the cost price argues no dim acquaintance between Buchanan and the whisky market – and the candid presentation of £175 to the customer is a most memorable feat of bona fide baksheesh. Buchanan had style. And 7,000 gallons out made room for 7,000 gallons in – of Buchanan Blend.

Buchanan was selling mainly in bulk, for consumption in public places. As the popularity of his whisky increased, it was necessary to put more of it up in bottles, suitable for the small home. (But it was remarkable that not only clubs and hotels, but many a stately home – or indeed any jumped-up *nouveau-riche's* mansion with cellar accommodation – consistently stored whisky by the butt or hogshead – respectively 108 gallons or around half that capacity.) Public approval was not slow in being expressed. The virtues of Buchanan's 'blend sufficiently light and old to please the palate' so impressed the author Frank Boyd that in his memoirs, published only thirty-five years after Buchanan founded his business, he refers to pre-Buchanan days as a sort of Dark Age. 'Scotch whisky of a drinkable sort was then a comparatively rare thing in England, and one still recalls the dreadful brass-cleaning concoctions which masqueraded under the style and name thereof.' Whether or not it was a fair judgement to compare a single malt whisky with an ostentatiously acid product like Brasso is a plea now lost in the obscurity of history, but the comparison still affords valuable sociological comment on the taste of 1885.

Buchanan produced his bottle. It was of black glass. It bore an attractive label with extremely graceful lettering. It announced:

The 'Buchanan Blend'
Fine Old Scotch Whiskies
suitable either for Grog or Toddy

The label did not last long. For the opportunity arose to present more impressive publicity. Buchanan pulled off a deal with the catering contractors to the House of Commons. During his first year of independent business, and in the face of what even he considered very keen competition, he secured a contract to supply Scotch whisky to the bars and cellars of the House of Commons. It was a swift and very appreciable advance, and Buchanan tapped all the prestige he could from it. It was a period when two forms of advertisement were then most convincing and acceptable, though they cut less ice today – the testimonial and the gold-medal award. or other prize, from an international exhibition. Buchanan secured a letter from the refreshment contractor, on House of Commons notepaper, declaring, 'The Buchanan Blend of Scotch Whisky you now supply to this Department is much liked by the Members and others who use it. It is with great pleasure that we express our high opinion of its quality.'

This was a testimonial of great impact, and it was a notable achievement to secure it for – not just a new variation in the first year of its creation – but what was virtually then a new product: blended Scotch whisky.

Buchanan used this impressive recommendation as vigorously as he knew how. But he was aiming higher. His plan was to secure a monopoly.

Within two and a half years, in April 1888, the London newspaper *Figaro* carried the following paragraph:

> *Madame Adelina Patti-Nicolini drinks exclusively at her meals Whisky and water; all orators and all persons who require to make use of their voice have adopted in this country this drink. It is therefore not surprising that the House of Commons submit to a severe test such an important part of their daily consumption as whisky. After comparison, it has been decided that Messrs James Buchanan & Co of Glasgow and London be the sole purveyors of it.*

At first sight, conceding that from the evidence of construction and vocabulary it was probably written by a recent convert from Esperanto, this was no strikingly new thing. It was a 'puff' of a style quite common at the time. Adelina Patti (she married, as her second husband, the Italian tenor Nicolini) was the outstanding opera singer of her time and had been London's favourite for twenty-seven years. Whether, at the age of forty-five, she medicated her vocal chords exclusively with whisky and water was a hypothesis no more worthy of serious investigation than any actress's public declaration that she never used any other than a named brand of toilet soap. Many corrupt journalists could get puffs of this nature into the editorial columns of the press, and often they canvassed manufacturers for money as payment for inserting the name of one brand rather than another. The *Wine and Spirit Trade Record* was sharp in detecting these puffs, and took some malicious pleasure in exposing them. The *Record* duly reprinted the puff from *Figaro*, with a suitably ironic comment. But what they failed to do was to deal with the astonishing last sentence. It implied that James Buchanan had an exclusive contract with the House of Commons, and this was an entirely novel situation.

The fact was astoundingly true. Buchanan did not bother to argue with the trade press. But in the next issue of the *Wine and Spirit Trade Record* – and in every issue for many years afterwards – he inserted a small panel-advertisement which quietly claimed:

James Buchanan & Co., Glasgow & Leith,
Head Office: – 20 Bucklersbury, E.C.
Sole Suppliers of Scotch whisky to the House of Commons.

Then Buchanan went to Paris and secured the gold medal for blended whisky at the international exhibition commemorating the centenary of the French Revolution.

This was a respectable achievement, equivalent today, perhaps, to winning one of the numerous annual Miss World contests. But the conquest of the Commons was indeed a triumph, and Buchanan converted his permanent publicity in accordance with it. He adopted House of Commons as the brand name of the Buchanan Blend, and this attribution now had pride of place on the label. The nomenclature held for over fifteen years, until in 1904 the phrase Buchanan Blend, which was now subsidiary to House of Commons on the label, was changed to Buchanan's Special.

But the public had the last word. For years they had reserved their own name for the Scotch, and particularly when casks began to yield to bottles on the shelves behind the bar. Buchanan's had always been presented in its distinctive black bottle with the white label, and increasingly it had been asked for as 'the black and white whisky.' When the first Trade Marks Act became law in 1905, Buchanan registered Black & White as his copyright description. He put the name on the label, at first in lighter type than House of Commons, then in 'Number One billing' over it. Finally he deleted the old brand name altogether, and the product was described and presented as:

Scotch Whisky
'Black & White'
Special Blend of Choice Old Scotch Whisky

with the autographed signature of James Buchanan & Co beneath. It is a rare example of a highly publicity-conscious man quite properly ceding to the decision of the ultimate arbiters of effective publicity – the public themselves.

Buchanan's close connection with the House of Commons, and

his instinctive skill as a lobbyist, were of the highest importance to the Scotch whisky trade over the next years. Buchanan, and the other dedicated promoters of his era with whom he was alternately rival and colleague, had come down for the principle of the massive exploitation of blended Scotch. It is impossible to say that they were right – only to note that they were highly successful. Professor David Daiches has observed that public taste can be created, that brilliant advertising and merchandising have largely created the popular palate, and that 'if the brilliant salesmanship that went into the marketing of blended Scotch whisky in England in the second half of the nineteenth century had been put at the service of the marketing of matured malt whisky instead, it might have had the same success.' Against that view, it can be put that, where the public taste has been given a free run, it has consistently favoured the bland as against the highly flavoured, whether the preference under review has been for marketed versions of whisky or horse radish sauce, or deliberately bred dilutions of veal, celery or grapefruit.

In the 1880s blended Scotch whisky still had its organized opposition from the malt distillers, which was not to be stilled for twenty years. On this issue any propaganda by Buchanan and his fellow-promoters was very acceptable. But the spirit trade as a whole was given an unpleasant and entirely unexpected jolt in 1885. Childers, the Chancellor of the Exchequer, imposed in his budget a twenty per cent increase in the tax on spirits, bringing it to twelve shillings a proof gallon. This was supposed to be a precautionary fiscal measure to finance a war with Russia, in Afghanistan, for the defence of India, which did not actually take place. It is interesting to note that, loud though the whisky men wailed against this tax, whisky was of so little social consequence at this stage that the general public saw the measure only as an attack on gin. The comfortable middle classes, who rarely drank gin, were prepared to accede to this as a diminution in self-indulgence among the working classes, whose beer was also to be more heavily taxed. Less complacent thinkers urged that the Horse Guards might at least help to pay for their own war by accepting an increase of three shillings and sixpence a bottle on champagne – which would have doubled the price. They elaborated:

The experiment might be tried as a feeler, and if hailed, as we feel sure it would be in every right-minded quarter, with enthusiasm, the field could soon be rapidly enlarged.

With a tax of, if necessary, five hundred per cent. on little dinners, diamonds, new hats, drawing-rooms, wedding-breakfasts, three-volume novels, dados, false hair, objets d'Art, footwarmers, prize cucumbers, Dukedoms, scented soap, foxhounds, Caviare, double-barrelled surnames and all the other accepted 'extras' of modern existence, the veriest Jingo could scarcely fail to face the grim 'circumstance of war', if not with absolute exhilaration, at least with some consciousness of its material expense.

In the event there was no war, Gladstone's government fell after losing the vote on the Budget, and the succeeding government withdrew the tax, which remained steady for twenty-four years save for two small nibbles to finance the Boer War.

Whisky was left, unchallenged for the moment by the

government agency of Customs and Excise. The war of the malt distillers, however, continued. By 1890 it was sufficiently sharp to justify the appointment of a Select Committee of the House of Commons which was to examine the fundamental justification of the modern whisky blenders who were introducing quantities of up to fifty per cent of patent-still grain whisky into their blends of malt and grain.

As with all select committees, the investigation was prolonged. But Buchanan certainly did not suffer from it. In a remarkable testimony, a medical man, Dr Bell, when called as a witness, paid unstinting tribute to James Buchanan himself as a pioneer of blending and a beneficent provider of the sort of whisky which the public now required. When the Committee finally reported, it gave blended whisky an admirable bill of health:

Certain distillers urged that spirits distilled in patent stills from malt and grain were entitled to be considered as whiskey [still the general spelling in legal references]; that they are used sometimes as such directly, and are now largely employed in blending with pot still whiskey. They gave evidence that there was increased demand for whiskey of a milder kind, and that blends of pot still and patent still whiskey were in large demand by consumers, who thus obtained a cheaper and milder whiskey containing a smaller quantity of fusel oil and other products. The blending or mixing of different kinds of spirits, chiefly whiskey, has now become a large trade. It is stated that public taste requires a whiskey of less marked characteristics than formerly, and to gratify this desire various blends are made, either by the mixture of pot still products, or by the addition of silent spirits from the patent stills.

Your Committee do not recommend any increased restrictions on blending spirits. The trade has now assumed large proportions, and it is the object of blending to meet the tastes and wants of the public, both in regard to quality and price.

As sole supplier of Scotch whisky to the House of Commons, Buchanan could be fully satisfied with the outcome of the parliamentary report, just as the House of Commons was apparently fully satisfied with his tipple. In the meantime he had been marching financially from strength to strength. The trade itself, in the decade from 1887 to 1897, doubled its production of malt and grain spirits. Then, in the typical end to a boom where the weaker speculators over-reach themselves and tumble, confidence ebbed swiftly, banks foreclosed on a large number of over-optimistic (or greedy) venturers, and the principals of the company which had led the runaway boom, Robert and Walter Pattison, were imprisoned for fraud. Buchanan did not falter in his stride, except to give an expert valuation of the Pattison whisky stocks at the request of Scottish bankers concerned – an invitation which he always remembered as a high compliment to his skill and integrity, since his was the only name the bankers would accept.

By this time Buchanan had extensive export interests. His London offices had become too small, and in one inspired night he bought the premises of the Black Swan Distillery in Holborn as his new headquarters. 'Where the money was coming from I had no idea,' he said later, 'but I was quite satisfied with what I had done. Inside of a week I had without any difficulty arranged my finance, and my business took a fresh leap forward.' The egocentric 'my business' is worth noting, for it was true. What was most remarkable about the operation was that it was conceived and approved in the notorious year of the 'Pattison Failures'. This gaily adventurous capitalist enterprise was still possible for an individual man whose personality and commercial record had earned the trust of the city. Buchanan, if he did gamble, played from strength.

In this, as in many other enterprises, he was immediately rewarded. He was promptly given the Royal Warrant of Appointment as Scotch whisky distiller to Queen Victoria. (Buchanan now owned the first of many malt pot-still distilleries to safeguard the constituents of his blend). The Prince of Wales, who rarely followed his mother in anything she had initiated, nevertheless capped the honour by bestowing his own Appointment, and when he became king soon afterwards he renewed the Royal Warrant.

Buchanan had his historic distillery in Holborn demolished, and commissioned a new edifice, a rather fanciful turreted creation of a style somewhere between Balmoral-baronial and Hans Christian Andersen, but certainly gayer than the huge carbuncle of the Prudential building opposite. He now had the yard space to indulge in his passion for horses – a genuine enthusiasm from which, as with the smart pony in the shining buggy of his early days, he saw no harm in extracting publicity. His beautiful vanhorses, all over seventeen hands high, daily paraded to draw a fleet of wagons crewed by coachmen and trouncers in a memorable, almost theatrical, costume which Buchanan had registered as a copyright design. This spectacular show was a daily part of London life for over thirty years. At his country estate, Lavington Park in Sussex, Buchanan was breeding race-horses. He had long ago ventured into the world of the turf as a race-horse owner.

From his new headquarters Buchanan whipped up world exports and created a small empire of branch offices within Great Britain. In 1903 he 'went public' converting James Buchanan into a limited liability company with £1 million authorized capital, but there was no public issue – the Governor had supplied all the capital. Shortly afterwards he bought out the business of his old friend Lowrie of Glasgow, who had staked him in his first independent venture in 1884, and had been repaid within a year. Lowrie himself had had a shaky time during the financial hurricane of the Pattison failures, and had been grateful to stretch out a hand in turn to Buchanan for steadying support. Now, at the age of seventy-five, he was glad to retire. Buchanan set his company up as a subsidiary with half a million capital. He built a new bonded warehouse and bottling stores, then bought a bottlemakers and a case-factory. After only thirty years in the trade which he had largely created, this tall, hard and confident man, as shrewd as ever and as spare of figure as ever, but with the red fading out of his hair, decided that business conditions had changed to a point where it was not profitable always for him to walk alone. He amalgamated with the Dewars under an arrangement whereby the two companies maintained their separate identities, but combined on joint measures of consolidation and expansion of their stocks and resources for the future. Ten years after the merger, Buchanan and Dewars and Walkers amalgamated with the Distillers Company Limited.

By this time Buchanan had become Sir James Buchanan, Baronet, and was later created a baron as Lord Woolavington, a title he held for thirteen years until his death in 1935. His wife could not share the honours. After twenty-six years of marriage she had died in 1918, through over-strain after nursing the warwounded in London hospitals. Buchanan sought his own consolation in increased activity and discriminate philanthropy – which was for the most part reserved until after he had been given his barony.

In one year, 1922, he experienced the award of his peerage, the marriage of his only child, Catherine, to Captain RN Macdonald, M.C., Scots Guards (later Major Sir Reginald Macdonald-Buchanan) and the winning of his first Derby with Captain Cuttle. He won again with Coronach in 1936. Lord Woolavington was then elected to the Jockey Club. He continued racing until his death, retaining his daredevil character, the dash, the nerve – which, strangely enough in such a combination, was remarkably inoffensive. Nobody seems to have borne a grudge against Buchanan, everyone warmed when they saw him. The stories told about him 'to illustrate his character' are legion. Sir Robert Bruce Lockhart tells one, and then says swiftly that it is not true. But Lockhart may protest too much because of the so-called 'shame' of getting mixed up in Lloyd George's Honours Traffic. Buchanan had the steel to go into such an encounter and emerge unsullied, even triumphant, having scored off the professional

[FAC-SIMILE OF ORIGINAL]

Refreshment Department
May 4th 1893

To
Messrs James Buchanan & Co.
Scotch Whisky Merchants
London EC.

Gentn
          I have very great pleasure in
bearing testimony to the high class quality
of the Scotch Whisky that you supply
to this Department and which gives the
greatest satisfaction.
          Herewith please find official order
for quantity at present required and
which be good Enough to forward at
your Early Convenience
               I am Gentn
               Yours faithfully
               William Aggas
                    Manager

Buchanan gets to the House of Lords
Radio Times/Hulton

hypocrite of the Liquor Controversy. The tale is that Lloyd George offered Sir James Buchanan, Bart., a peerage, at the price of a stiff contribution to political funds. Buchanan grimly agreed – and, as a gesture marking his distrust of Lloyd George, chose his new title and signed his cheque 'Woolavington', so that it could not be cashed until his peerage had been gazetted. No harm in that. Buchanan had publicly earned his honours in any case.

A more apposite story, in view of the identity of the next whisky baron to be discussed, concerns the rivalry between Jimmy Buchanan and young Tommy Dewar. One thousand licensed victuallers from the United States came to England for a convention-plus-holiday. Dewar, recognizing them as potential importers, gave them all a banquet. Buchanan then asked them to a far more sumptuous banquet, for which he hired the Crystal Palace. Courteously, he invited Dewar, who made one of his memorable after-dinner speeches. The leader of the American victuallers responded to the toast of the evening, 'We have enjoyed ourselves very much on our trip. The things we shall remember most in England are Victoria Vat and Dewar's Extra Special.'

He had mentioned two of Dewar's whiskies. Buchanan collapsed in his chair. 'Dewar has done it again,' he said. 'We have spent £5,000 for nothing.'

Thomas Dewar
Courtesy of Dewar archive

CHAPTER THREE

The Public Life of Whisky Tom

TOM DEWAR himself would not deny that he was a provocative character. It was all part of being a superb publicist, and of all the whisky barons he was instinctively the most skilful advertiser. Amusing things seemed always to be happening to him, and if they didn't, he saw that they did – and communicated the occurrence to the nearest newspaper. On his first world trip to drum up business, his itinerary included Quebec. As he recounted the sequel:

> When I arrived in the city, a Commission was sitting to consider the advisability of applying Prohibition to the whole of Canada. Some of the wild teetotal papers took me rather severely to task because I had the temerity to send in to the Commissioners some statistics showing the average life of various classes of drinkers; amongst them being the total abstainers, who had the shortest average, and the habitual drunkard, whose average was two years longer! The remarks of these teetotal literary gentlemen did me no harm; I wasn't mobbed, neither was there any attempt to lynch me.
>
> Prohibition has been tried in several parts of Canada, but has not found much favour. I may mention a rather amusing

Dewar's advertising
Courtesy of Dewar archive

experience here. I was going through a 'Prohibition' State, and tried to get some whisky from the conductor of the train, but without success. 'Can't do it, boss; we're in a Prohibition State, and I can't do it.' However, he eventually advised me to try at a store at the next stopping place, and this I did. 'Do you sell whisky?' 'Are you sick, mister, or got a medical certificate?' 'No.' 'Then I can't do it. See, this is a Prohibition State, so I can't sell it; but I reckon our cholera mixture'll about fix you. Try a bottle of that.' I did, but to my great astonishment received a very familiar bottle, which, although it was labelled on one side 'Cholera mixture: a wineglassful to be taken every two hours, or oftener as required,' had upon the other side the well-known label of a firm of Scotch whisky distillers, whose name modesty requires me to suppress!'

Thomas Robert Dewar was generally able to tap reserves of ruthlessness which enabled him to overcome that modesty. He came to London at the age of twenty-one on a single-minded mission to make the name of Dewar's whisky well known. He accordingly stormed the Brewers' Exhibition which was then held annually at the Agricultural Hall in Islington. He took a stand, though he was the only whisky promoter to do so. As soon as the exhibition was officially declared open, a loud and unmistakable sound hit the ears of those who were grouped round the ceremonial platform. It was a fierce call to arms spewing from the bagpipes of a very brawny Highland piper whom Dewar had hired to garrison his stand. The brewers rushed towards Dewar and shouted through the tumult their insistence that the noise should stop at once. Dewar refused. He had previously checked that music was permitted, and he stoutly maintained, necessarily at the top of his voice, that what they were being treated to was better than the oompapa-oompapa of a German band extolling a dubious lager, and that no finer paean of praise could be devised than the Scottish bagpipes accompanying the offer of a Scottish product: the name was Dewar, and would they care to place small orders now? Occasionally throughout the duration of the exhibition Dewar was bought off, if only to stop his bagpipes for a time. But the tactic of getting his name known proved successful, and at the next Brewers' Exhibition there was another stand alongside Dewar's – that of the watchful Jimmy Buchanan.

These two men had much in common and were clearly destined for long and serious rivalry – though they managed to keep it friendly for most of the time – but some of their circumstances were very different. Buchanan was fourteen years older; he was an entirely self-made man who had set up his whisky business only a year earlier, after getting five years' experience of London as agent to another whisky merchant. Dewar was a very young man who had had a slightly easier start in life, although during his painful acclimatization in London he was even more of a lost innocent than Buchanan. 'When I came, I had two introductions to possible customers,' he was fond of saying. 'I found that one was dead and the other had just gone bankrupt.' He told Hannen Swaffer:

'On the first Sunday that I was in London I went to a Presbyterian church. There was a rich man in the congregation who said to me, "If I can give you any advice, I will." I said to him, "I'm told you export whisky to India. I've got some to sell." He asked me, "How do you know that I export whisky to India?" I said it had come to me ears, and it was true, and since he had been good enough to offer me advice, I was repaying him the gesture by offering him whisky. He seemed annoyed at the way the conversation was going as we stood outside at the end of the service, and he said, "I'm sorry, I never mix religion with business." So I don't know what sort of advice he was intending.'

'And what did you do?' asked Hannen Swaffer curiously.

'I changed my church,' said Tom Dewar.

He was referring to the building rather than the sect. He had indeed been brought up within the close confines of the Scottish Kirk by a careful father. John Dewar, a crofter's son from Aberfeldy, on the River Tay in Perthshire, took work in his cousin's wine merchant's business in Perth, and eventually became a partner. In 1846 he set up on his own as a wine and spirit merchant in the High Street of Perth. He was the first to put up his own whisky in bottles, proudly labelled with his name, blends which his own judgement ruled to be suitable for his market. He married later and had seven sons, not all of whom survived infancy. The boys were educated at Perth Academy, and the second and fifth survivors, John Alexander Dewar and Thomas Robert Dewar, born when their father was fifty and fifty-eight respectively, were trained for the family business. John Alexander went to Leith, which was then the thriving centre of the Scotch whisky trade, and at the age of twenty-three was admitted as a partner to his father. Thomas also spent some time in Leith, and moved on to a sort of apprenticeship in Glasgow. But his father died when he was sixteen and he speedily came back to the family firm to help his brother. In 1885, when he was twenty-one years old, he became a partner and was sent south to wake up England.

He began with little more than lightning raids, as at the Brewers' Exhibition, backed by concentrated campaigns to gain introductions to useful people, with whom he left an overwhelmingly expensive quantity of samples. He did not open an office until 1887, when he took a small place off Cockspur Street, within a bottle's flight of Dewar House in the Haymarket which he later established as the company's uniquely memorable headquarters. But when he went into Cockspur Street his name was so little known that the landlord demanded the rent in advance. It was only twenty-one years before Dewar House was opened, but it is fair to say that, even many years before that landmark, Dewar was the most cheerfully recognized name in London, if only because Tom had collared the most effective solo site for illuminated advertising in the world – and had sent in his electricians to make the most of it.

He had acquired, as an interim head office and bottling centre, Dewar's Wharf, on the south bank of the river near Waterloo Bridge. The site included the 200-feet high Shot Tower, at the top of which molten lead had been poured through a sieve, and became hardened into lead shot as it dropped down into a tank of water below. Up the massive north face of the tower Dewar 'drew' with coloured electric light bulbs – a gay Highlander above whose bonnet the name of the firm blazed out. The action of the programmed electric circuit made the Scot pour out and drink innumerable glasses of Dewar's, while his beard and kilt fluttered in the wind. All who saw it still smile affectionately at the memory of its impact. For sentimental social historians it still stands for the great days of the warm, *personalized*, unskyscrapered London of that lively generation of what may be called the *Strand Magazine* era, stretching from Sherlock Holmes to PG Wodehouse, from hansom cabs to MG Midgets, for ever orchestrated by the hum and swish of the trains along the Embankment. That was Tom Dewar's London.

He laid out his massive empire, as has been said, within the twenty-one years enclosing the opening of his first and last London offices. But, in contrast to the achievement of Buchanan, this was not a one-man job. There were two Dewars in at the start, and more were to follow. Tom Dewar was the front-man, the witty and talkative salesman of quite compulsive charm, who became first an adoptive Londoner and then a dedicated globe-trotter – the Dewar export missions throughout the world have always been a remarkable feature of the activities of the house. But the firm could never have exploited his volatility had it not been for the steady back-room work of John Alexander Dewar, his elder brother, John Alexander Dewar of Perth. Perth was the still centre of his world – he devoted unlimited voluntary labour to the welfare of his birthplace, was City Treasurer for five years from the time when Tom began consolidation in London, was Lord Provost for a further stretch of six years, and then went into Parliament. He was the serious, even dour, businessman who transferred Tom's miracles of salesmanship into the organized achievement of production and delivery.

In this he was immeasurably aided by the skill and flair of a man who is still revered in knowledgeable Scotch whisky circles

– Alexander John Cameron, whom he brought into the firm shortly after Tom had established himself in London.

Cameron revolutionized blending, and all the leading houses unhesitatingly annexed his methods. It is not always realized by the 'malt missionaries' of pot-still whisky – who were vociferously rebellious at the end of the nineteenth century and are a perhaps better-justified cult today – that the malt whisky on offer in the 1880s, which blended whisky convincingly overcame in the world market, was not necessarily immaculate merely because of its pot-still origin. Some astonishingly immature whisky had been put on sale, and even when malt whisky had been 'vatted' (products of varying years and sometimes doubtful maturity, mixed in one cask), the blending had not always been done with the devotion of, say, a grand chef analytically testing his sauce at every stage of its construction. If 'sedentary' Victorians did get stomach-ache from malt whisky (though it is difficult to call any Victorian 'sedentary' in the face of the incitement of door-to-door sitting offered to today's whisky-drinkers) it could occasionally be ascribed to the casualness or ignorance of the distiller who had sold the product. Alexander John Cameron exploded that approach. He had a perfect nose, and fine judgement. He was an indefatigable experimenter. He evolved, over a lifetime, an art of blending. His copyists could hardly be restrained from, nor blamed for, catching the main principles.

Cameron established a truth about the individuality of whiskies: that harmony between various distillations is not consistent. Some get on well with each other as soon as they are blended, some need time to adjust, some ought never to have been married at all. Consequently, the process of blending – regardless of the flavour and bouquet you are finally seeking – cannot be crude. Dewar's have forty separate whiskies in their White Label blend. Alexander John Cameron and his successors did not pour them breakneck into a vat like punch. It was a matter of preliminary combination, order, and above all time. No British rubber-planter on local leave in Singapore, and no rancher ordering Scotch in Venezuela, could be expected to possess a technical appreciation of the finesse that had gone into preparing a bottle of Dewar's: the flavour and bouquet would be all that concerned him. So Cameron had to work towards approval by a distant, unseen customer, even if Tom Dewar had been around recently, putting on the influence when the call came for Dewar's. That was the length and depth of Cameron's achievement.

But Cameron did not have the standing, and Tom Dewar in his earlier years did not have the solidity, which were absolutely necessary in cold commercial terms to back the astonishingly swift progress of the partnership. Tom built up the promise of a remarkable metropolitan and export trade, but it needed rock-steady confidence to back it and this could only come from hard-headed external financiers. Foreign trade particularly demanded long credits. The combination of John Alexander Dewar's stolidity and Tom's sparkle secured these. At one period the Dewars' bank overdraft was £300,000 – twice the amount of their authorized capital when they first became a private limited liability company. But they fulfilled their commitments and justified the risk.

The time was the hey-day of exultant enterprise, the last fling of private capitalism. But nobody was 'on to a dead cert' – the decade of the triumph of the Dewars was also the period of the Pattison failures. Possibly the brothers possessed a special advantage arising from their close connection with the city of Perth – a link always maintained, even by Tom, who became an English country gentleman in Sussex like James Buchanan, but donated the priceless lung and beauty-spot of Kinnoull Hill to the royal burgh. A Dewar trait which is one of the imponderables in assessing their success is their intense family loyalty. John Alexander and Thomas Robert called themselves *John* Dewar and Sons, although the father had died a year before Tom came into the business and five years before his brother made him a partner. When John Alexander was raised to the peerage as Baron Forteviot, he took as his baronial motto the Latin phrase *Pro rege, lege, grege* – 'For the King, for the Law, for the Clan'. But when Tom became Baron Dewar, he took as his armorial motto *Gloria Patri*. It was an ancient and pious enough phrase. Translated as 'Glory be to the Father' it was the conventional ecclesiastical catchword for the old doxology. But Tom could appreciate a play on words, and was not ostentatiously religious. If he was claiming that his title was a belated honour to his own father, that was not inconsistent with his character.

It is also true that Tom Dewar put up as the crest for his baronial coat of arms a scarlet cock crowing from a bed of thistles. It would be difficult to represent more adequately a flair for publicity based on sound Scottish acquisitiveness.

He applied these talents as he made his prepared assault on London in the 1880s. It was a man's London then, compared with what it is now, particularly in the commercial sector. One or two self-conscious female adjutants could be encountered who were capable of operating the new-fangled correspondence machines – it was the girls, at that time, who were called typewriters. At the Albert Palace in Battersea Park there was even a Viennese ladies' orchestra on show – but peeping toms reported that behind the skirts much of the brass and percussion was being played by men, of whom the beefiest and beeriest were confined to the wings. As Dewar trotted round with his samples and a repertoire of funny stories that perhaps were more fundamentally suited to the masculine ambiance in which he moved, he had occasionally to submit to having his baggage searched. For there were bomb scares then, as now; the terrorists of the time were known as the dynamiters.

Tom Dewar's first major success came when he secured an exclusive contract to supply Scotch whisky to the firm of Spiers and Pond. The agreement provided admirable publicity, since this firm had a great number of catering outlets which included the railway station buffets. Dewar was also keeping up with Jimmy Buchanan, for although Buchanan had taken the music hall bars in the London theatres managed by Newsom Smith's United Music Halls, Spiers and Pond were also established in the entertainment world and had a high reputation for their catering service. When they took over the Albion, a theatrical tavern in Drury Lane, a London poet was moved to welcome the revival in words which give some hint of the pub life of the period:

Ho! Waiter at the Albion,
Before you bustle out,
Just put a juicy chop upon

The grid, and bring the stout.
For well you know me I'll be sworn,
Not one of your chance comers,
I've used this house both night and morn,
For five-and-forty summers.
How often in this room I've sat,
On many an afternoon,
And played 'mid histrionic chat,
With meditative spoon.
And oft at night I've talked and laugh'd
And scorned the winter's fury,
And haply modest beakers quaff'd
With actors from Old Drury.

The shadows of a by-gone age,
My dreaming eyes behold,
The mighty men who trod the stage
in all the days of old.
I see Macready and the Keans,
Here presently assembles,
Each hero of a thousand scenes,
Your Garricks and your Kembles.

And coming down to later times,
I see amid the smoke,
How Sothern heard the midnight chimes,
And Buckstone cracked his joke.
While actors of the modern school
Are here, of fame deserving;

Our Bancroft, and our lively Toole,
  And Hare, and Henry Irving.

And here, on many future nights,
  When some new play is o'er,
Will critics gather 'neath the lights,
  And actors throng the floor.
May each piece in those days beyond
  Our ken, find firm defender:
And well we know, O Spiers and Pond,
  Your chops and steaks are tender.

With trade increasing, and the newly joined Mr Cameron taking over the blending, the Dewars acquired the first of many distilleries in order to ensure their supplies. It was at Tulliemet, south-east of Pitlochry, and was leased from the Duke of Atholl, but its use was discontinued after a few years when the brothers built a new malt distillery at Aberfeldy, near their father's birthplace. They were making marked headway as bottlers of blended whisky, and had taken their first gold medal in that class at Edinburgh as early as 1886. As has been said, exhibition medals were then taken very seriously as awards of merit, and therefore misleading claims were prosecuted with zeal. In 1891 Dewar's won a court action against an Edinburgh wine merchant who claimed in his publicity that at a recent international exhibition he had won 'the highest prize, the gold medal, for the superiority of his blend over the whiskies of all other competitors from every part of the Kingdom'. He had indeed won the gold medal, but at that particular exhibition the first award was a diploma of honour which was taken by Dewar's, and the wine merchant had not therefore won 'the highest prize'. Once the action began, the defendant retracted in a statement which Dewar's refused to accept, and the judge, finding against him, said that John Dewar and Sons were entitled to the publicity which the judgement afforded rather than an acceptance of the private withdrawal and apology which had been offered.

The reach of publicity is incalculable. Shortly after the judgement, the following letter reached the partnership:

> *Kingussie, N.B.*
> *Cluny Castle, September 21, 1892.*
>
> *Messrs John Dewar & Sons,*
>   *Merchants,*
>   *Perth.*
>
> *Gentlemen:*
> *Can you get a small keg, say nine or ten gallons, of the Best Scotch Whisky you can find, and ship it addressed as follows:*
>
> > *To the PRESIDENT,*
> > *The Honorable Benjamin Harrison,*
> > *Executive Mansion,*
> > *Washington, D.C.,*
> > *U.S.A*
>
> *Send bill to me.*
>
> > *Yours very truly,*

The signature was of Andrew Carnegie, the Dunfermline-born American millionaire from railways, oil and steel, who was coasting into retirement and an old age as a Scottish laird while he planned the philanthropy he was about to embark on – he donated over £10,000,000 to endow public libraries alone. Carnegie wanted to provide a treat for his 'special friend', the President of the United States, and Dewar's accordingly sent their White Label. Within a year, Thomas Dewar was standing in the White House, and assuring a rather dubious major domo that there was something of his in the cellar. Dewar had taken it into his head to set his whisky on the shelves of the leading cities of the globe. He was in the middle of a non-stop world tour – continuous travel and virtually non-stop talking. He was away for two years, visited 26 countries, and returned with 32 firm agencies established.

It could be justly rated as an impetuous decision. A proposition of a two-year stay away from the centre of exploitation had a certain air of unreality about it. It could only have been fulfilled with bountiful cooperation from the Perth end of the business. But London, which had been so assiduously tilled, could not be left without a harvester. Tom Dewar left his office boy. This was a marvellous period for the recognition of promising youth, but one can only say that Dewar must have been a superb judge of character. For the young man, Fred Whitfield, subsequently became a director – and one certainly earned one's rank as a director in the Dewar organization.

Dewar's judgement of character was, in fact, to be justified in more than one direction. Many of the firms he appointed as agents in 1892-3 held their connection with the firm for fifty years. And it was while Tom was away on tour that the partnership (not even yet a private company) received the Warrant of Royal Appointment to Her Majesty Queen Victoria as Scotch whisky distillers. Tom may have had an influential hand in arranging that honour. But Fred Whitfield, ex-office boy and future director, can hardly have let the firm down while he held the fort in London.

John Alexander Dewar had gone into local administration in Perth. Thomas Robert Dewar went into local politics in London. In March 1892 he stood in only the second election in history for the London County Council, which had been formed three years before. John Alexander Dewar was a Liberal all his life. Thomas Robert Dewar, aged twenty-eight, stood with a more experienced colleague as a Moderate (which in London meant a Conservative) against the Hon & Revd Canon Leigh and Edward Markwick, barrister-at-law, who were Progressives (which in London meant Liberal). There were fewer than a hundred votes separating the candidates, but Dewar and his friend were successful. Almost immediately he went abroad on his business tour, which, if it took two years out of the three he served in office, can hardly have commended itself to the electors of Marylebone West.

He set sail from Liverpool in the *City of Paris* for Queenstown (now Cobh) and New York. From the beginning he discovered that he had some difficult proselytizing to do, in two directions.

We had a service on board on Sunday, when an American missionary of the Moody and Sankey type delivered a very long oration about civilising the whole world, speaking very modestly of his own countrymen, and contenting himself with saying that Americans were improved Englishmen once removed. The steward told me before landing that the sale of

Irish whiskey had been double that of any voyage during the past twelve months, and said he accounted for it from the fact of there being six Irish priests on board.

Soon after leaving England we had all burst into song, and given vent to our feelings by singing 'God save the Queen.' As we approached New York, much to my surprise, it was sung again with redoubled vigour. I liked this feeling very much, and remarked on it to a young American lady whom I had befriended during the voyage. But, to my astonishment, she stared at me. "What, can't you tell the difference between your own National Anthem and 'Land of Freedom'? Tune's the same, but the words are altogether different. Guess you want to say we don't speak plain!" I was in a state; but, 'pon my word, the nasal twang stopped me from hearing the difference.

Dewar was prepared to do as much sightseeing as the next tourist. But he was engaged on a hard sales trip, and he had made all possible preparations. 'I was treated right royally wherever I went,' he reported, 'and was made an honorary member of most of the best clubs. These clubs are very elaborate affairs, and far more gorgeous than those we are accustomed to on our side.' Dewar baulked, however, at the gorgeousness of the cab fares, which he calculated were a dollar minimum. 'After that I gave up cabs, and threw in my lot with the millionaires and the niggers by always using the "street-car". The fare is very moderate. Five cents will take one anywhere.'

After a whirl of business engagements, Dewar took the Blue Line train to Washington for more business. 'I had my first

Perth office staff, 1895
Courtesy of Dewar archive

The Blending Room at Perth
Courtesy of Dewar archive

experience of dining on the American cars. It was not at all a bad experience either. To be sure, the crust of the claret got stirred up a bit; but what did that matter? We were travelling about fifty miles an hour.' He thought Washington a beautiful city, with Parisian boulevards along which ran electric cable-cars, 'smoothly and quietly at from twelve to fifteen miles an hour'. He went to the Capitol and the White House.

Much to the surprise of the patriotic official who showed me over the White House, I was able to tell him something about what it contained. He was expatiating proudly on the fact that everything, or nearly everything, was American-made, when I mentioned that he must not forget that there was something from Scotland in the cellar. At first he looked hurt; but when I gave him my card, and he saw who I was, his countenance relaxed, and the meaning smile which beamed over it proved that he was as well aware as I of what had travelled from Perth to Washington some few months previously.

Dewar returned to New York via Baltimore and Philadelphia, and then sailed to Newport, which he called New York's Brighton.

The 'Sassiety' there is said to be extremely select. The 'Four Hundred' is particularly so, and is looked upon – by the members – as the créme de la créme of an exalted aristocracy. Yet, after all, what is it? The only qualification is the almighty dollar; and so long as this is possessed to an inordinate extent, and the ladies are able to smother themselves with diamonds, the end is attained; the greater the amount of dollars and diamonds, the greater is the respect shown to the possessor. But are the natives of Newport alone in this particular? I think not. Still, the affair is carried to such an extreme there, it is impossible not to view it from its ludicrous side. For instance, the mansions, or almost castles, of which the place chiefly consists, are called cottages; and the cottage which Mr Vanderbilt has erected completely puts Solomon's Temple in the shade. This cottage is said to have cost several million dollars, and it certainly looks like it. It is built of pure white marble, and I was informed every stone was obtained from Europe.

Bathing is a very favourite amusement here. I stayed at the Ocean Hotel, a large residential hotel, and capitally conducted. However, I had not been in the place half an hour before I came to the conclusion that there were too many doors about. Upon my arrival I was conducted to my room, and thereupon arranged my toilet for dinner. When this ordeal had been completed, and I was about to leave, I noticed there were two doors in my room. I opened the one I thought I came in at, but it led to a bathroom, which was occupied by a lady wearing the same costume as Eve before the fall! With an incoherent apology, I beat a hasty retreat, the lady saying, 'Guess I ought to have seen that door was locked.'

Dewar moved on to Boston, where he found the population priggish, so much so, he said, that when the first Bostonian died and told St Peter where he came from, he was told 'That's a bit difficult. However, do come in; but *please don't be disappointed!*' Nevertheless, even in aristocratic Boston, Dewar picked up an advertising gimmick of the Jimmy Buchanan genre. At an opera first night the front row of the dress circle was occupied by young gentlemen wearing cloaks over their evening dress. When the prima donna appeared, they threw back their cloaks to display gleaming starched shirt-fronts bearing the slogan: 'Do you wear pants? If not, go to So-and-so's Pant Company.'

He moved on to Portland, Maine, which he found depressing because of its local Prohibition rule, and from there to Quebec, where he attracted the publicity already mentioned for putting his statistics on the average life of various classes of drinkers in to the Prohibition Commission then sitting there. He moved through Canada to Niagara, and south to Pittsburg, but did not visit the steel plants of his acquaintance Andrew Carnegie on account of the local difficulty caused by a strike, which the Pennsylvania Militia had been called out to quell. He moved on to Chicago, where he was disconcerted by the ubiquitous spittoons, but was able to quote a gem of an instruction discouraging graffiti in public cloakrooms. 'In gold letters on the top of a beautiful marble slab are the words, "Gentlemen wishing to show their artistic ability will please use the left slab for pictures and the right for poetry; signatures at foot".' Dewar then travelled north again to Canada and went west by train. In the Rockies he found settlements of Scottish crofters 'who have one very bad habit: they *will* distil their own whisky'. In British Columbia Dewar actually conversed with the engine-driver of the train in Gaelic.

His next stage was to get to San Francisco, from where he took a ship for Honolulu. There were a number of missionaries aboard, and one of them gave him the publicity he always cheerfully welcomed:

A Scottish teetotal parson tried to improvise a service on deck, and gave an address. He had evidently been foraging around amongst the officers and list of passengers to know who and what everybody was; for, when talking of the vessel on which we were as a sort of ark, and all that sort of thing, he drew comparisons of the people on board, and amongst others was: 'We have missionaries on board going to convert the heathen, and we have a heathen grog-seller on board going to convert the civilised to the evils of whisky-drinking, and encourage those who are already wallowing in that degrading and pernicious vice!' Good man! I didn't pay him anything for the advertisement, although at the time I wondered whether he would expect anything. I must say, however, that my feelings were very considerably hurt by being called a 'heathen'! I, who had been brought up most strictly in the tenets of the Shorter Catechism, the Scottish Kirk, and porridge, to be called a heathen!

Honolulu, Samoa, New Zealand: here Dewar rediscovered the delights of an old passion by taking the ribbons and driving a coach on the long journey from Auckland to Napier. He also, for the first and only time in his candid confessions, fell in love, with the niece of the landlord of the Tarawera Hotel. But he refrained from sending any *billet-doux* to the lady concerned, living up to one of his most famous 'dewarisms' – 'Do right and fear no man; don't write and fear no woman' – which was fortunate, since he discovered that the girl was engaged to the coachman whose reins he had taken over for the journey. He rid himself of some of his chagrin by swinging into activity and milking the hotel-keeper's cows, another unsuspected talent which he had retained from his boyhood. Eventually he resumed his journey, and dropped down to the outskirts of Napier.

Fields of corn and hay were all around; sheep stations, looking like young mansions, after what we had been used to for some time, were dotted about; but the greatest sign of return to civilisation was a school that we passed just at 'coming out' time. Fine specimens of young New Zealanders these youngsters were. Strong, healthy-looking lads and girls, freckled and bronzed by being so much in the sun and fresh air, and with a free and happy look upon their faces that was quite enjoyable to see. There were a dozen or more ponies about the school door, and these we were told belonged to those who came from a distance, some of the scholars coming seven, eight and nine miles to school. We cheered the youngsters and they cheered us – in fact, we felt almost like schoolboys again ourselves; and then we stopped and took as many of the boys on our coach as were going our way, starting off again with tremendous cheering from the coach party, the cavalry and the foot scholars.

Dewar sailed south to Christchurch, where he already had contacts, and he enjoyed 'a rollicking time'.

To wind up everything I gave a dinner-party, and I really thought this was never coming to an end. Everybody had a toast to propose, not only connected with those present, but of whatever they could think of. Loyal and patriotic toasts were uproariously received; frozen mutton was greeted with cheers as vociferous as those for the Queen. Early in the morning this jovial party broke up, but the last was not heard of it. I had one or two pressmen amongst the party [trust Tom Dewar!] and the morning papers contained a long account of the whole proceedings, embellished with many flowery additions. This was too much for the teetotal faddists of the place, and next evening they held a special meeting in one of their halls to protest against what I had said [in praise of Dewar's White Label] and a gentleman of the name of King orated himself hoarse in an address, the subject of which, he said, was 'Mind your own business'; and if words had had any effect I should have been dead a dozen times, and pulverised out of recognition. Most earnestly he besought the young ladies of the place never to think of marrying any but total abstainers, and strenuously exhorted every one to join him and his brethren in their work of 'trying to sweep away the mischief caused by those who sold whisky'.

Gentle, kind-hearted man, to trouble himself so much on my behalf. I didn't want to marry anybody ...

Tasmania, Hong Kong, Canton, Shanghai, Japan. The sales trip went on inexorably. The full itinerary reads: New York, Washington, Baltimore, New York, Newport, Boston, Portland

(Maine), Quebec, Montreal, Ottawa, Toronto, Niagara, Buffalo, Oil City, Pittsburg, Cleveland, Detroit, Chicago, Minneapolis, St Paul, Winnipeg, Moose Jaw, Banff, Glacier, Vancouver, Seattle, Tacoma, Portland (Oregon), San Francisco, Honolulu, Samoa, Auckland, Roturua, Whakarewarewa, Taupo, Tarawera, Napier, Wellington, Christchurch, Dunedin, Hobart, Melbourne, Sydney, Port Darwin, Timor, Hong Kong, Canton, Shanghai, Nagasaki, Kobe, Osaka, Kioto, Tokyo, Yokohama, Shanghai, Hong Kong, Saigon, Singapore, Colombo, Aden, Port Said, Alexandria, Marseilles, Monaco, Nice, Paris, Calais, Dover.

The important non-European territory omitted was South America, southern Africa and India. South America demanded, and received, a special visit. Dewar had already, in his short period of salesmanship, been more than once to Natal, the centre of British influence then, and had established an agency at Madeira en route. As for India, after the small disaster of the Indian merchant who would not talk business on Dewar's first Sunday in London, India had been accounted for after a small corrective action.

Dewar had changed his church.

Now it was back to London and dynamiters. On the very first day that Tom Dewar arrived in London from Perth there had been a serious bomb explosion on London Bridge which, he had joked, had not really been caused by terrorists but by 'Macaulay's New Zealander', who was getting impatient. The reference was to a passage in Macaulay's *Historical Essays*, more famous then than now.

The Roman Catholic Church 'may still exist in undiminished vigour when some traveller from New Zealand shall, in the

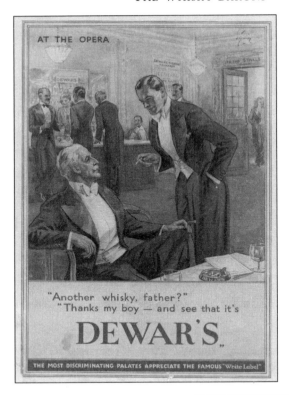

Dewar's advertising
Courtesy of Dewar archive

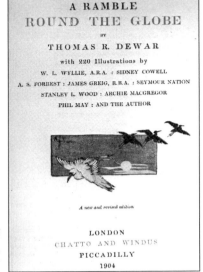

The title page of
A Ramble Round the Globe,
London 1904

midst of a vast solitude, take his stand on a broken arch of London Bridge to sketch the ruins of St Paul's.'

It was Dewar's joke that Macaulay's New Zealander had been waiting for so many years to see the ruins that he had become impatient. 'I can't wait till I'm an Old Zealander, I'm a Middle-aged Zealander as it is.' Now, amid the sentiment of reaching London again, he retracted some of his cynicism and showed how massively, before he had reached the age of thirty, he had defected to the South:

Once more I go out into the streets of the greatest and most marvellous city on this earth, to be assailed with the true London cries that fall almost as music on the returned wanderer's ear, 'Piccadilly, 'Yde Park, 'Ammersmith,' 'Paper, extira speshul, all the winners,' and the other old familiar cries, and to see once more the bustle and the rush which is simply unequalled in its genuineness! Yes, I am at home once more; and the substantial superiority over everything I have seen, which seems to pervade the very air, comes before me like a flash. Republics, kingdoms, empires, all are good; but Old England beats the lot, and London (ignoring Macaulay) says as with Tennyson in 'The Brook':
'Men may come, and men may go, But I go on forever.'

If the Perth end of John Dewar and Sons had harboured any doubts about the salesmanship, the export efforts and the public relations charisma operated by Tom Dewar from the London end of their enterprise, all hesitation had vanished by the time he returned from his world trip, when the first orders he had

The London Office of Thomas Dewar
Courtesy of Dewar archive

solicited had already come in. Sales were rocketing. Prestige was high. They had the Royal Warrant. In 1894 they transformed the partnership into a private company, and three years later they quadrupled the capital – and saw with satisfaction that the public were willing to take £250,000 worth of preference shares at a ten per cent premium. In 1896 they began to build the Aberfeldy Distillery, and the next year Tom Dewar became the youngest Sheriff of the City of London, while John Alexander was still serving as Lord Provost of Perth. At the turn of the century they had passed the million gallon-a-year production total and were building new vats solely for blending which held 6,000 gallons apiece. In 1900 both brothers became Members of Parliament – John Alexander as a Liberal for Inverness-shire, a seat he kept for sixteen years, and Thomas Robert as a Conservative for St George's in the East which he lost in the Liberal landslide of 1906. In 1901 Mr 'TR Dewar was elevated into knighthood.

Sir Thomas Dewar was an Accession knight. The honour had been bestowed by King Edward VII, who had just come to the throne, and it was a mark of personal favour, for Tom was moving in royal circles now. For some years he had been able to afford to indulge his natural interest in high sport, and to an extent this had drawn him towards the then Prince of Wales. In 1895 Dewar acquired what was said to be the third motor car bought in Britain: the Prince of Wales had the first and Sir Thomas Lipton the second. The machine was a $3^1/_2$hp chain-driven Benz, and its highest running cost was for teams of horses to tow it home. In 1897 Dewar put up his racing colours and, with the beginner's luck that never deserted him, bought

Forfarshire, a horse which came third in the Derby: the Prince of Wales won the Derby in 1896 and 1900. But there is no doubt that Dewar's closest connection with the new king came through their mutual intimacy with Lipton. He was a Glasgow boy who had emigrated to America, then returned and started a provision shop in Glasgow. His business prospered and he opened shops all over the country. Then he bought tea and coffee plantations in Ceylon and finally ran a whole grocery-production chain which extended to an abattoir and packing-station for hogs in Chicago and a bacon-curing plant in England.

In 1897 Tommy Lipton went full-toss into big sport, particularly into the most expensive pastime of all – big yacht racing, which even the Prince of Wales had had to give up because of its cost. But Edward and Lipton became great cronies. Three times in Edward's lifetime, and three times later, Lipton challenged for the America's Cup with his yachts *Erin* and *Shamrock*. He was unsuccessful in every contest.

Tom Dewar and Lipton – who was knighted in 1898 and made a baronet after the Accession – were wonderfully warm friends. They were known as 'the two Scotch Toms'. Dewar accompanied Lipton to America for the yacht-race challenges and supported his friend in the after-dinner speeches for which he was now famous – though he managed to sell a great quantity of whisky on his trips, too. They maintained a remarkably extravagant bantering relationship. Dewar once went into a Lipton shop in Harrogate and announced that he was an inspector from Lipton's head office and he was to make a thorough investigation of the shop. After he had been shown all over the premises, he announced that he was so satisfied with the way the business was being run that every member of the staff would be given £1 a week rise in pay. Naturally, the episode came to Lipton's ears, but he would not cancel the increase. 'I went on paying,' he said.

On a sales trip to Central Africa, Dewar sent Lipton a cable. It ran: 'You can buy three wives here for six pounds of Lipton's tea. Why not come out?' Lipton immediately telegraphed back: 'I am sending out the tea. Send samples of wives.' They were both bachelors.

The two of them were in Taormina, Sicily, with Kennedy Jones, an associate of Lord Northeliffe who had worked with him in founding the *Daily Mail*. 'We are certain to find the paper on sale here,' swore Kennedy Jones. Dewar disagreed. 'You'll have as much chance of getting the *Daily Mail* here as Lipton would have of getting a pound of his tea.' Jones searched the town for his paper but could not obtain it. Dewar, rising to a challenge, combed the place for a bottle of White Label but, to his great chagrin, could not get one. Then he asked for a packet of Lipton's tea. It was immediately produced. 'One up to Tea Tom,' said Lipton.

Lipton told a damaging story of Dewar's experience as an East End Member of Parliament – the St George's in the East constituency was the modern Tower Hamlets. He took the Liberal Chancellor of the Exchequer, the Hon CT Ritchie, to address the electors. They had a splendid meeting which was suddenly swept into disaster when it was found that the Chancellor's overcoat had been stolen from an ante-room. Dewar kept the company talking there while he sought out his agent, gave him a sovereign, and asked him to make every effort with 'the boys' to get back the Chancellor's coat quickly. Ten minutes later a whole selection of stolen coats was brought in, and one – not the best, said Lipton – was recognized as the Chancellor's. A few nights later, Dewar revisited his constituency, and a committeeman complained bitterly to him of the bad way in which he had been treated over the lost coat. 'Why?' said Dewar, 'I gave a sovereign for its safe return. Wasn't that enough for an old coat?' 'A sovereign!' wailed the committeeman. 'What a swindle! I only got a bob for it from your agent – *and I was the bloke who pinched the coat!*'

Another crony of Dewar and Lipton was the comedian Harry Lauder, also knighted. Lauder used to spend much time at Dewar's great estate, Homestall, near East Grinstead in Sussex, where he went into bloodstock breeding on a grand scale – involving himself not only in race-horses, but in greyhounds (he won the Waterloo Cup for coursing, again characteristically at his first attempt, with a dog called Winning Number which he said he had bought for a ten-pound note and only because of its name) and in pigeons and poultry, goats and pigs and waterfowl. The horse of which Dewar was fondest was Abbot's Trace, who showed terrific speed in the Derby and was leading after a mile, when he collided with another horse and fell. The horse was thought to be dead, but he got to his feet and was walked back to the paddock. Dewar was deeply disappointed, but resisted all advice to sell the animal. He bred many fine horses from him, winning over £250,000 in stake money. They included Abbot's Speed, Abbot's Smile, Abbot's Remorse, Abbot's Frown, and Dewar was criticized by a racing journal for registering these similar names, with the comment that the situation was as bad as it had been when a horse called Bachelor's Button was almost duplicated in name in many of his descendants. Dewar wrote to the editor of the paper claiming that surely an Abbot had as much right to boast of his progeny as a bachelor.

Harry Lauder, who was a canny man, spent an afternoon at Homestall extravagantly praising Dewar's pigeons in the hope that Whisky Tom would give him some for his own estate at Glen Branter, in the West Highlands. Dewar yielded to the hint, and promised to send up a pair of his best birds. 'Here's a better idea,' said Lauder. 'In case you forget, I'll just take them with me. I am going up to Scotland tomorrow.' Dewar agreed, Lauder telegraphed his estate manager to prepare a pigeon cote. With some difficulty Lauder bundled the birds in their basket on to the train for Scotland, and duly installed them. Next morning they had disappeared. Dewar had given him homing pigeons.

Tom Dewar had an amused, provocative wilfulness in his nature which apparently assumed that his 'fee' for the after-dinner speeches he was constantly called upon to make was a reference – as dutiful as the flattery in a Loyal Address – to the sovereign quality of Dewar's White Label. Even when he himself was the host, he did not dodge this duty, as he enunciated his mélange of repartee and encomium with a slightly hissing, Churchillian delivery. When Sir Harry Lauder returned from a triumphal engagement in the United States, Dewar arranged a welcome-home banquet for him, and naturally made the speech of honour. 'Harry Lauder and Dewar's whisky are the greatest cementers of Anglo-American friendship,' he declared. When, at another dinner party, he did not fully catch the name of the lady by his side, she repeated very distinctly 'My name, if you please, is Porter-Porter, with a hyphen.' Unabashed, he replied, 'Ah, just as mine is Dewar-Dewar with a siphon.'

His flair for publicity was matched with his passion for sport in the great series of Dewar Cups and Dewar Trophies which he initiated for almost every sport, from association football to bowls. He was the first patron of sponsored sport, and did not limit his activities to the home country. In South Africa today they still compete for Dewar Trophies for rifle-shooting, soccer, bowls, yachting, pigeon racing and even fire-brigade efficiency. The Dewar Golf Shield there was presented as long ago as 1903.

But Dewar's greatest prestige, and probably Tom's keenest delight, came from the club-like atmosphere of the ground floor of Dewar House in the Haymarket, which was in his day the rendezvous for every sort of celebrity from cabinet minister to matinée idol but *also* – and this was (and is) its delightful unexpectedness of sociability – the 'pad' where Dewar's expected and even demanded a call from 'their man' in Singapore, Sydney or San Francisco whenever he was in town. Dewar collected a notable work of art for this headquarters. Tearful Scots will want to touch the tavern table from Ayr on which Burns wrote many of his poems. But no one needs sentiment or patriotism to react to the Dewar masterpiece, the portrait of *The MacNab*, painted by Raeburn in about 1810 – the grandest delineation ever achieved of a wilful, warm Scot – whether Whisky Baron or Colonel of the Breadalbane Fencibles.

Tom Dewar himself was a painter manqué. He had sufficient control of line to be able to send postcards from America to Sir Thomas Lipton with no name and address, but only a caricature of Lipton. But his own, more modest version of his efforts was that, having painted a cow in a meadow and asked a friend for an opinion, he was told, 'The ship seems all right, but I think you have made the sea too green.'

John Alexander Dewar had leapfrogged Tom and become a baronet before the Great War came. Early in the difficulties of this crisis, Dewar's and Buchanan amalgamated, allowing themselves much unilateral freedom. Dewar had always said 'Competition is the life of trade, but the death of profit', and perhaps this union might loosen the noose. The merger brought Tom Dewar, of course, into much more intimate contact with Jimmy Buchanan, against whom he had sparred and schemed for thirty years, to the great disadvantage of neither. They were both great whisky promoters, but highly dissimilar in almost every other characteristic, from Buchanan's giraffe-like neck to Dewar's settling cosily on his shoulders. One of Dewar's soundest observations was 'No two people are alike, and both of them are glad of it', but the two separate distillations blended well in the new vat.

In 1917 John Alexander became Baron Forteviot, and his brother advanced to baronet, and then in 1919 Thomas Robert became Baron Dewar. There was no underhand influence about it, even though the honours came from Lloyd George – or Tom, at least, would surely have spilled it. It was another of his aphorisms that a secret is either not worth keeping or too good to keep. Buchanan joined them as Baron Woolavington a little later. They came together out of the war – 'A new world is being born,' said Tom, 'and judging by the noise, it's twins' – and soon went into the merger with the DCL and Walker. Tom Dewar continued as an urbanely cynical public commentator, 'Nowadays people arc miserable because they can't get the things their forefathers never had. Traces of civilization are reported to have been found in the most remote corners of the earth ... so that's where it has gone; Man's greatest task today is to keep straight and yet make both ends meet.' But he took care always to cap a crack with praise of whisky.

He continued in the public image as a sporting country gentleman, a shrewd man about town, but above all as a whisky magnate. He never let up on his salesmanship. He never stopped his export drives. When the *Lusitania* was sunk by a German submarine in 1915 she was carrying home a Dewar staff man reporting back. Since 1902 Tommy Dewar had had in the field another Dewar, but no relation – Peter Menzies Dewar, who, presumably under the whip of Tom's exhortation 'A Scotsman is never at home unless he's abroad', spent nearly thirty years as a world salesman, going round the globe eight times and making nearly one hundred trips to the United States. (In the early nineteen seventies. Dewar's could name only Albania, China and certain strict Moslem sheikdoms where the inhabitants could not get White Label – unless they were invited to a party at the British Embassy!) When the two pioneer barons, John Alexander and Thomas Robert Dewar, died within six months of each other in the winter of 1929–30, PM Dewar took over the chairmanship. John Alexander had sons to follow in the firm, and the present Lord Forteviot, is now chairman. Thomas left his fortune and his sporting enthusiasms to his nephew John Arthur Dewar, son of his brother Charles who had never come into the firm. But John Arthur Dewar had had what Tom called, with a remote American pun, a dour training in the export business, had created the company's extensive South American interests, and had three trips round the world on his own tally. He later became chairman of the firm, after dutifully winning the Derby with Tom's horse Cameronian. It is remarkable how John Dewar and Sons Limited, a very integral founding fatherland and federated kingdom in the DCL whisky condominium, still manages to retain the structure of an old family firm. And a call at Dewar House still conveys the impression that one is going into the London home of Thomas, Lord Dewar – deceased, but surely not now resident very far from Haymarket and the bustling London he had given his heart to. Tom had had a good life, and, in essentials, a simple life. He used to say that a man's reputation depends on what's not found out about him. But, when the posthumous gossips and biographers reached for their magnifying glasses, there was precious little unrevealed to find out about Whisky Tom.

The Sheriff of London, 1897
Courtesy of Dewar archive

CHAPTER FOUR

Alcohol is Purer but not Superior

THE FIERIEST OF ALL the pioneers of modern-blended Scotch whisky was Peter Mackie, the 'father' of White Horse. From the point of view of the traders, who were angrily divided before they reached a final harmony, Mackie was at times a dangerous propagandist. For he had a puritanism of thought which impelled him to pursue his logic to the end of the argument, even when it pained the more commercially minded of the patent-still grain distillers. He had a foot in both camps – owning one famous malt distillery and building another, but using the product of the large grain distilleries for his blend. Yet he attacked the 'young, cheap, fiery whisky' – by implication, immature grain products – 'responsible for most of the riotous and obstreperous behaviour of drunks', and prompted ferocious head-shaking among the company directors who disposed of it. The only explanation of his conduct – which even his enemies accepted – was his insistence on high quality, which no disgraceful hobby-horse to ride. In the end, his uncompromising stand was of great benefit to the quality and reputation of Scotch whisky.

Peter Jeffrey Mackie, who gloried in his Highland blood, was born in 1855, which made him six years younger than James

Winston Churchill and James Stevenson
Courtesy of Diageo Archive

Buchanan and nine years older than Thomas Dewar. At the age of twenty-three he joined the partnership then run by his uncle, James Logan Mackie, which owned the Lagavulin Distillery on the island of Islay. He went to Islay immediately, to begin his education. Islay lies in the Atlantic, off the west coast of Scotland beyond Kintyre. Its whisky has always had the most pronounced flavour of all Scottish malts. It is generally described as 'peaty', but peat is used in the drying of the malted barley for all malt whisky, and Mackie always said that his water, which had run from two lochs over a hundred waterfalls before it reached his distillery, had passed over a bed of moss as well as peat, which gave it its distinctive flavour. At any rate, Lagavulin whisky was individual enough in its own right to be bottled and casked as a single malt whisky, and exported long before the whisky boom of the last quarter of the nineteenth century. The flavour of Lagavulin, nowadays somewhat over-ridden to suit the more bland requirements of today's consumers, can still be distinguished in White Horse.

The company responded to the increased world interest of the 1880s by producing blended whisky. By 1891 Peter Mackie was virtually the sole director of the private partnership now called Mackie & Co. (Distillers) Limited, had built on Speyside, in the Highlands, Craigellachie-Glenlivet distillery, and had registered the name White Horse. Slowly – for he was not moving at the same speed as the young giants – be became able to open offices in London and Liverpool and to pursue an aggressive export policy.

In the beginning it was only the export trade that was profitable, and indeed not until 1901 did White Horse become available on the home market as a bottled, labelled blend subject to the comparisons and demands of the public taste – not that Peter Mackie had any great regard for the discrimination of the British public at that time. For later chroniclers, Mackie is the most candidly revealing of all the whisky magnates because, as head of the important Craigellachie Distillery, he made public statements on the commercial disposal of malt whisky which inevitably shed light on the progress and prospects of blended whisky. When his shareholders proposed that he should bottle and sell Craigellachie malt, rather than sell it in casks only for blending, he revealed details of the disappointing launch of White Horse on the home market. His (White Horse) company had 'four years ago put on the home market a brand of the highest age and quality, second to nothing that had ever been offered to the public. They expected to make a large profit, but they had been disappointed.'

The reason he gave was that 'they had not calculated the immense sum required for advertising, owing to the ignorance of a large section of the English public in regard to quality. The result was that we dropped nearly £80,000 in that venture. Luckily we had good business elsewhere, otherwise it would have been a serious affair.'

Mackie went on to cast aspersions, not only at public taste but catering companies' rackets:

There is a section of the public who know quality, but there is a larger section quite indifferent, who are only influenced by extravagant and persistent advertising. In addition, a large number of caterers demand heavy premiums before they will sell such high class brands as I am speaking of, and even then do all they can to discourage the sale of such brands by charging an extra price on them – so that they may push their own bulk whiskies, from which they get more profit, quite irrespective of their reputation for quality or of the good of the public.

Mackie then became controversially involved in the three-and-a half-year long controversy around what is now called the 'What is Whisky?' question. It began with the zealous officials of a local authority, the Islington Borough Council in London. Their inspectors became concerned with enforcing the Food and Drugs Act. They first moved against sales of so-called brandy. The main effect of the phylloxera scourge on the vineyards had long since receded, but the trade practices which resulted from the serious diminution of brandy stocks had not been extinguished. Brandy had been adulterated with grape juice and neutral alcohol, and this unpalatable and sometimes dangerous mixture was still served in many public houses. Consummating the busy activities of their inspectors, the Islington Borough Council had successfully prosecuted a number of local publicans for selling brandy 'which was not of the nature, substance and quality demanded by the purchaser.' They then turned their attention to whisky.

On the assumption that whisky could be produced only from a pot still using the fermented mash of malted barley, the Islington inspectors toured the pubs of the borough, asked for whisky, and analysed what they got. In every case, where they had not asked for malt, they found traces of grain spirit. To be truthful, they found much more than what would scientifically be called 'traces and when they experimentally asked for malt they were not in- frequently given a blend of malt and grain, but they proceeded on the simple request for 'whisky'. The Islington Borough Council took out a summons as a test case, and the stipendiary magistrate of the North London Police Court ruled that the publican concerned had not given whisky when he was asked for it, since on analysis the potion contained a proportion of patent-still spirit. By case-law it was therefore the fact, until the decision was reversed, that blended scotch whisky was not whisky because it contained a proportion of patent-still grain spirit, which was an adulteration under the Food and Drugs Act.

Naturally, there was consternation in the booming blended whisky trade, and some more-than-sly smiles among the rearguard of malt distillers who maintained that God was a spirit emanating principally from the Highlands. The Distillers Company Limited, who at that time were concerned only with grain spirit, financed an appeal, but when it was heard over many sessions by a King's Counsel sitting with lay magistrates the Bench was evenly divided and no decision was laid down. Therefore the original magistrate's judgement stood.

The patent-still interests, who then governed what was quantitatively the great majority of the trade, put it out that the matter was in *sub judice* limbo – which, in fact, it was not for a long time – and the Distillers Company bravely brought out and widely advertised their own guaranteed Scotch-grain patent-still whisky distilled at Cambus, north of the Forth between Stirling and Alloa. 'Light, delicate, exquisite', they proclaimed with some spirit since they boldly called it whisky, 'seven years old,

Lord Stevenson at the closing of the Wembley Exhibition, 1925, with the Duke of York (later King George VI) and JH Thomas, Secretary of State for the Colonies, with Colonial High Commissioners.
Radio Times/Hulton

matured in wood, NOT a pot still whisky', though its price was the same at three shillings and sixpence a bottle. 'The Whisky with an individuality – notably different to all others in peculiar delicacy and charm of flavour – mild and yellow. A soft, round, natural, wholesome stimulant, that ministers to good health and neither affects the head nor the liver.' They finished their declamation with the fanfare, 'Not a Headache in a Gallon' and the picture of a man in persuasive evening dress hoisting a toast glass which contained at least a gill.

The feverish endeavours of the grain distillers and the blenders clashed, as would be expected, with the law's delays, but two-anda-quarter years after the original decision by the magistrate a Royal Commission was set up to determine what, if any, rules should be applied to the production of whisky and whether a minimum period should be fixed for maturing it.

Mackie, who was never bothered by any declaration of *sub judice*, did not hesitate to comment on the topic, but he took a completely independent line. Of the magistrate's original decision he said:

> *I think it will be the means of the public's getting better whisky, because the brewers will buy better whisky for their tied houses than what they have bought in the past. I am not so much concerned with whether the whisky is pot-still or patent-still. If only the whisky is sufficiently mature, and it is made by sound methods, I do not think the means by which it is made matters much.*

Maturity, quality, age ... those were the criteria Mackie was always pressing for. He asseverated, 'What the public wants is age and plenty of it. Better value in Scotch whisky is given today than at any time in the past, if only the public ask for the right brand.'

He favoured a minimum of three years in the maturing of any whisky to be sold to the public, and said the reputable blenders would welcome it. 'People engaged in the better-class trade would favour a three-years minimum. But very few want a veto on patent-still spirit. Had the trade in whisky been confined to malt, unmellowed by grain spirit [the use of the word 'mellowed' is significant here, for Mackie was not a hypocrite for commercial purposes, and other people besides himself have indicated that some malt spirit was raw] the trade would not have been a tenth of what it is today. Nine out of ten drinkers of Scotch whisky prefer their whisky with a quantity of old grain in it. It seems to soften and improve the blend, and bind it together.'

While the judicial authorities were still deliberating, other authorities made up their minds. White Horse whisky soared to the peak of its exhibition career by gaining the Grand Prix at the Franco-British Exhibition in 1908, and the achievement was crowned by the announcement of the Royal Warrant to Mackie's company as distillers of blended Scotch whisky. Next year the Royal Commission tardily backed this judgement. In a massive overturning of the legal position to that date they refused to 'recommend that the use of the word "whiskey" should be restricted to spirit manufactured by the pot-still process', and gave it as their general conclusion (in phraseology that lasts to this day) that "whiskey" is a spirit obtained by distillation from a mash of cereal grains saccharified by the diastase of malt; that "Scotch whiskey" is whiskey, as above defined, distilled in Scotland.' The only change (in effect, a narrowing) of this definition was made after sixty years in the Finance Act, 1969, which added the conditions that the cereal mash should (a) 'have been fermented by the action of yeast, and (b) have been distilled at less than 166.4° proof in such a way that the distillate has an aroma and flavour derived from the materials used, and which have been matured in wooden casks in warehouse for a period of at least three years.'

The Royal Commission of 1909 had rejected this three-year

maturation. It may have been their innocence or ignorance, but by the time they reported, this issue was unexpectedly vital to those in the whisky business who demanded quality, and the Royal Commission had played into the hands of the disreputable end of the trade. For the Chancellor of the Exchequer, David Lloyd George, had introduced a controversial budget (which took fifteen months to pass) declaring a war on poverty and imposing a thirty-three per cent increase in the tax on whisky. Lloyd George was an acknowledged public enemy of the 'Drink Trade', and drew many nonconformist votes from that professed allegiance. But Peter Mackie fought him publicly on every relevant issue in the budget. He declared it the product of:

a faddist and crank, and not a statesman. But what can one expect of a Welsh country solicitor being placed, without any commercial training, as Chancellor of the Exchequer in a large country like this? I might as well bring into my business and place at the head of it a bootmaker or shoemaker or country solicitor, and any man will know how incompetent he would be for the job.

Mackie then proceeded to beat Lloyd George on his own ground:

if it was nationwide thrift the Chancellor wanted ... there is only one remedy to retain the self-respect of the British people ... and this is Universal Compulsory Old Age Pensions, with contributions paid one-third by the worker, one-third by the employer, and one-third by the State. This would encourage thrift and be the finest temperance movement that this world has ever seen, and do more to encourage temperance and thrift than all the prohibitive notions that ever have been introduced by cranks and so-called temperance fanatics.

The effect of the budget, Mackie declared, was simply a fifty per-cent drop in the sale of high-class whiskies. 'Cheap, immature whisky in many cases has taken its place, and is being pushed without any regard to reputation. The great mass of the public, ignorant of the quality and unwilling to complain, is the victim. A scheme of graduated duty would assist the sale of old whisky.'

This scheme of graduated duty was Mackie's pet idea. It was a carefully worked out proposal to substitute for the budget increase on whisky a scale of decreasing duties according to the age of the whisky. Spirit under six months old would be charged Lloyd George's full impost. ('As no one admits to using new spirits,' said Mackie cunningly, 'no one could object to this increase.') Whisky over six months and under two years old would pay slightly less duty, whisky under three years old less again, and so on until whisky over five years old paid at the standard rate before the increase.

It was a reasoned proposal, in the best interests of the quality trade, and Mackie twice interviewed the Financial Secretary to the Treasury on the subject. But the grain distillers fought the proposal vehemently, and went to the Chancellor himself. Mackie made a public reply which came near to splitting the industry wide open:

I shall be perfectly frank and explain my position. I am a malt distiller, but I am also a shareholder in the Grain Distillery Company ... [the protest to the Chancellor] is drawn up by grain distillers, whose product is the cheapest class of spirits in the market, and, although chemically purer than malt, as they state, and which I quite admit, yet it is principally used when aged for blending with malt whisky. But, when new, it constitutes the chief whisky for the cheapest and lowest-class trade in the poorest public houses. Alcohol is a degree purer than grain whisky, but that does not give it a superiority over malt whisky, as those grain distillers claim for their grain whisky. No one thinks of drinking pure alcohol.

As regards the alleged purity of grain whisky as compared with malt whisky – scientific authorities have established the fact that it is the so-called impurities, ie, the ethers and higher alcohols and by-products in the malt, that are the valuable properties for medicinal purposes, but it is necessary that they should be matured ...

It is in the interests of the working man, many of whom are not judges of whisky, that they should be protected from the young, cheap, fiery whisky which is offered. Experience teaches that most of the riotous and obstreperous conduct of drunks comes from the young and fiery spirit which is sold, while men who may over-indulge in old matured whisky become sleepy and stupid, but not in a fighting mood.

The argument went on for over a year, but Mackie lost that particular round. Eventually he won his campaign for matured, quality spirit – though not for graduated tax, which was merely a ploy to induce that objective. But Mackie did not win entirely on his own, and he had to wait until a major war before he found his ally.

That ally was James Stevenson, later Baron Stevenson of Holmbury. Stevenson was a Johnnie Walker man in the days before that company sold Johnnie Walker, which does not mean before 1820, when everything started going strong. It is true that in 1820 John Walker set up in Kilmarnock as a grocer and wine and spirit merchant. From 1856, with his son Alexander helping and inspiring him, he began blending whisky, principally for sale to the foreign merchants who came to Kilmarnock to buy its noted carpets, and to Glasgow sea captains who indulged in private trade once they had delivered their official cargo in foreign ports. Alexander Walker opened an office in London in 1880, and introduced three sons into the firm. When he died in 1889, his third son, Alec Walker took command. The next year James Stevenson, a Kilmarnock lad, joined the staff. It was not until 1908 that Stevenson moved to take over the London office, and in that year 'Johnnie Walker' was created by the artist Tom Browne, who had been given a portrait of old John Walker and was asked to devise a poster based on it. Until then, the firm's whisky had been sold as Walker's Kilmarnock Whisky. As Johnnie Walker, with Browne's fantasy-creation, it became the largest-selling whisky in the world.

How much the success of a well-advertised whisky is due to its recognized quality, and how much to the cosy recognition of its image, is a judgement which few whisky blenders, and even fewer advertising wizards, would care to pontificate on. Peter

Mackie depreciated public judgement, and purported to despise advertising yet he (rather than Jimmy Buchanan, who might be assumed to have an equal claim) sued a German firm that was selling whisky as 'Black & White Horse'! The top prize and gold medal in public wooziness must go, however, to the gentleman who wrote the following letter:

Messrs. Dewar & Co., Glasgow.
Dear Sirs,
    I have very much admired your poster of two cocker spaniels, as I have one exactly like them, and should like a copy. We always drink your White Horse whisky at home here.
Yours truly

Dewar's headquarters are at Perth. The dog poster is of two Highland terriers, not spaniels. It is issued by Buchanan's. And White Horse is Mackie's whisky.

It was James Stevenson who, with George and Alec Walker, pushed Johnnie Walker to the top of the league. When the Great War came, Stevenson was co-opted by Lloyd George to coordinate the newly created Ministry of Munitions, although Stevenson had previously referred to the Minister's efforts as those of 'the blustering, humbugging interference of a temperance minority which thinks it is going to abolish thirst'. Lloyd George was still indulging his Prohibition obsession, and was determined to ban all whisky distillation for at least the duration of the war. It was only the propinquity of Stevenson, whom he greatly trusted, that convinced him of the truth that, without the by-products of distillation, there would be no yeast to bake the country's bread, no alcohol to produce high explosives, no fusel oil to coat aeroplanes with dope, no constituents for anaesthetics.

Winston Churchill said of Stevenson:

Among all the ablest business men, striving under wartime pressure to do their utmost for the country, [Stevenson renounced all remuneration for the duration of the war] he was always first or among the first ... Not only did his special department for the supply of guns and shells far exceed all previous records or expectations during the period of his control, but in the general work of the Munitions Council and in the adjustment of difficulties inseparable from the strain of wartime administration, he showed the qualities of a business statesman and leader of men. My own obligations to him are endless.

Stevenson himself, with the collaboration of Mackie, countered Lloyd George's proposal of total abolition with a ban on the consumption of the almost raw alcohol – permitted since the Royal Commission Report of 1909 – which was undoubtedly paralysing and demoralising the munitions workers. Stevenson declared, 'I am the real author of the Immature Restrictions Bill. It was I who suggested to the present Prime Minister [Lloyd George] when he was Chancellor of the Exchequer, that "All spirits should be kept in bond for three years".'

Stevenson, as has been said, eventually became a baron. Peter

Mackie was gazetted a baronet, and Alec Walker, who had also abandoned his firm to serve the Ministry of Munitions, was created a knight. Stevenson's most memorable comment on the Immature Spirits Act, which Mackie had for so long campaigned, was, 'There is no greater enemy of Pussyfootism than good liquor.' And there is no better introduction to the next episode in the saga of the Whisky Barons.

CHAPTER FIVE

Whisky or a Crown of Glory?

THE VEHICLE MOVED SEDATELY past the face of Buckingham Palace, where the band still played *God Save the King* for George V. It turned into the Mall and then left towards St James's Palace, and ignored the curses of taxi-drivers and draymen to pull up outside the ancient casement-windowed front of 3 St. James's Street.

'That ain't the side the Limeys drive,' growled the man in the back.

'How else do I get you where you want to go?' asked the driver.

'Is this it?'

'This is it.'

It proclaimed itself, in discreet lettering running along the base of its flagstaffed balcony, to be Berry Bros. & Co., with an even more discreet reminder that the firm was, by appointment to HM the King, Wine Merchants. The place reeked of courtliness and rare vintages. Its aura throbbed with tone.

Two men left the car, glanced quickly to right and left, and made way for their chief to get out. They pushed open the door of Berry's and stared distrustfully into the atmospheric interior.

It was a Dickensian prospect of dark panelled walls and high desks, with a rolling wooden floor contoured like the sea in a long swell in Rum Row, an unsteadying deck of a floor which in comparative age might have seemed almost Shakespearian – if the visitors had been able to identify either Dickens or Shakespeare.

Francis Berry looked up from a place at the back of the Coffee Mill, as the ancient shop was still named. He saw three shapes in broad-brimmed fedoras, their hands ominously thrust deep into their topcoat pockets, and recognized the types, if not the faces, instantly.

An immaculately suited assistant moved towards the visitors.

'You see that sedan outside?' asked the principal.

'Yes Sir,' said the assistant, politely if not accurately. Bred in the traditions of the firm, he would not have been unduly surprised to have seen a sedan chair beyond the windows where, a century and a half earlier, the Quality had emerged from many such conveyances while the chairmen waited outside.

'How many cases can you load into her?'

'Cases, Sir?'

'Of liquor. Hard liquor. Genuine Scotch.'

The assistant looked again and saw only a closed car.

'Into that saloon?' he asked.

'Is this a saloon?'

'No,' said Walter Berry, the other partner in the firm, moving smoothly forward. 'This is not a saloon. This is a merchant's house.'

'A liquor merchant's?'

'A wine and spirit merchant's.'

'Like I said,' the leader of the visitors confirmed. 'We've come to do business. How many cases? ... '

'Mr? ... ' asked Walter Berry.

'Diamond.'

'Legs Diamond,' said an escort in a voice combining proprietary pride and professional menace.

'From Chelsea,' his partner added.

'Oh, Chelsea! ...'

'In the Bowery,' came additional confirmation in a growl that had never lisped in Eaton Place.

'Good morning, Mr Diamond,' said Walter. 'I think you should meet my partner, Mr ... '

'Sssss!' came a warning hiss from Francis Berry, already beating a tactical retreat as he mounted the stairs out of the main office.

'What are you interested in?' resumed Walter Berry with the utmost urbanity.

'Liquor. I wanna place an order.'

'A shipping order,' elaborated one of his bodyguards.

'How many cases can you stack in that sedan?'

'Perhaps fifteen,' hazarded Walter Berry.

'I'll take three hundred.'

'Cases?'

'Scotch.'

'Now?'

'Tomorrow.

'Payment?' queried Walter Berry. 'On delivery.' said Legs Diamond.

'Where?'

'Here. Tomorrow morning. Ten o'clock.'

'Cash?'

'Cash. I take it you'll cut in a discount.'

'Not on such a minimal order,' said Charles Berry firmly.

'Minimal schminimal. Did you say criminal?'

'*You* said criminal,' Walter Berry corrected him. 'Will you bring your own, er – sedans?'

'Cabs,' said Mr Diamond. 'Twenty cabs, tomorrow morning, ten o'clock. Do we get to sample the product?'

'You haven't specified the product yet,' said Berry with severity. 'Scotch. Your own Scotch. Berry's. The nobs go for it. Do you have more than one?'

'We have four,' said Berry primly. 'Perhaps you would take a glass of this?' And he motioned to an assistant who poured three glasses for the visitors. 'Would you like water with it?'

'What do you take me for?' asked Legs Diamond, and he swigged his drink. 'Not much kick in it, is there?'

'What do you want? FISH-HOOKS?' hissed Francis Berry across the ceiling from his observation post below the first-floor landing.

'Pretty label, though,' conceded Diamond, and he lowered his head and his voice as he projected a powerful stream of halitosis into Walter Berry's face. 'A dollar a dozen for twelve thousand labels,' he proposed with overpowering urgency.

The blast of ulcers-and-garlic was turbulently stopped in full flow by a force-twelve 'PTCHAH!' erupted from the mortified but still actively indignant depths of Charles Walter Berry, fifth of that line and probably the most puritan of all those generations of wine merchants in his devotion to the family product. 'PTCHAH!' the tempest raged once more. 'I hope I can take it, sir, that you are joking!'

'Joking, of course,' said Legs Diamond, visibly shaken and not yet certain whether Berry wanted more money or total silence on the subject of labels.

'Because this company is PAYING,' continued Walter Berry, 'paying good money for warning notices in the American press stating that the labels of Berry Brothers and Company are being forged, that they are often affixed to bottles of poisonous methyl alcohol, and that especial care should be devoted to ensuring the veracity of anything bearing our label, since we have consigned no wines or spirits to the United States since the year 1917.'

'Wonderful!' said Legs Diamond in admiration. 'What great publicity. If it's yours, it's good. 'Cos if a drop is sold, it's six years old.'

'Sixty-five years old, if you refer to our Grande Fine Champagne, said Berry didactically.

'You hear that, men? French champagne, sixty-five years old.'

'It's Cognac, brandy,' said Berry with some venom.

'It should be,' said Diamond, keeping his end up as best he could.

'Well, if this is the liquor the lords like ... Say,' Diamond interrupted himself with a new thought and pushed his glass at Berry. 'Does the King drink this?'

'That matter is entirely confidential.'

'The Prince of Wales, perhaps?'

'I'm afraid it is not your business. May I ask what market you intend your order for?'

'Not your business,' rolled a ghostly echo along the ceiling.

Walter recognized the voice of his partner, and spoke swiftly to close the deal. 'Tomorrow morning at ten, then,' he said.

'Payment on delivery,' said Diamond, and he forestalled Walter Berry as he saw him opening his mouth to speak. 'Cash,' he confirmed, and jerked his head at his bodyguards and withdrew. The saloon car was nonchalantly turned against the tide of the traffic, and rolled past the guards at St James's Palace carrying far more armament than was entrusted to the sentries.

'Thanks, Walter,' said Francis Berry emerging from his upstairs retreat. 'I didn't care to handle that one. He's a character I might be thrust against in Nassau, and I don't want to be slapped on the back as an old friend.'

'If that's the type you meet in Nassau, I'm glad to stay at home,' observed Walter. 'Legs Diamond. Why is he called Legs?'

'He was a champion ballroom dancer. His only civil grace, as far as I know. You got a bit near the knuckle with your minimal-criminal.'

'Is he?'

'He's been arrested about a dozen times, but he has never been convicted. Generally works a discharge before trial. He must have a magic touch with the police. Well, that's not strictly true. He served a year in Fort Leavenworth for deserting from the American army when the bugles sounded Charge. Had one sentence for theft as a juvenile, too.'

'What *is* he?'

'He seems to be spreading his wings. He's a hoodlum in the protection racket, really. Said to be very handy with a gun. Can't quite make out what his game might be. There's no doubt he's in the bootlegging business once the stuff is ashore, but a bootlegger isn't a rum-runner. In spite of his fancy legs be could hardly stand up on our floor, let alone on a schooner off Nantucket Island. In any regard, 300 cases is very small beer for a rum-running shipment.

He could be trying his hand, joined a syndicate to stock one of these freighters they're always talking about setting up as floating warehouses. You're not giving him any Cutty Sark, are you?'

'Good lord, no.'

'Absolutely right. Cutty Sark has got to start clean. Untainted. Totally reliable. And the best guarantee against adulteration is to work only through Nassau.

Francis and Walter Berry, the two partners then running Berry Brothers and Company with the junior partner, Hugh Rudd, were in reality second cousins, both being great-grandsons of the wine merchant George Berry, who had come up from Exeter over a century previously to enter the family business at 3 St James's Street bequeathed by his mother's father. Of the two partner-cousins, Walter, short and stocky with a profoundly religous devotion to wine, rarely left the Coffee Mill except to go on foraging trips through the vineyards of Europe. Francis, tall and lean and almost jumping with nervous activity under his calm exterior, was the company's ambassador and pleni-potentiary, displaying a familiarity with steamship and railway timetables almost as impressive as his enthusiasm for wine.

His travelling trunks bore the labels of hotels in thirty countries in the five continents, irrevocably fixed with the tenacious glue of the period. His baggage 'not wanted on voyage' had to be carefully stowed, delicately retrieved, and

These 'torpedoes' were found on the schooner *Rosie MB*, filled with
Scotch malt when a United States destroyer captured the ship. A
flotation chamber allowed the torpedoes to be towed ashore just
under the surface when small craft ran the liquor ashore.
Radio Times/Hulton

handled with gentle reverence. This man was indeed an
ambassador, bearing costly gifts from a distant country in the
shape of his samples of wine. He was also, sociologically, a
commercial traveller, a salesman, bagman or drummer – which
he freely conceded on social occasions, though not omitting the
dry observation that the Prince of Wales was in the same line
now that he had begun his goodwill tours to North and South
America and other parts of the world. Francis Berry was not a
snob. It was not his own importance he recognized so much as
the importance of his product. He had an enthusiasm for good
wine which he seemed bursting to pass on. But at the same time

he was fastidious and correct to an almost comical degree of English tradition. At a medium level of intimacy, one quality tended to compensate the other in its effect on a customer. A self-conscious *nouveau riche*, or a Colonial carrying a slight chip of an inferiority complex towards the Old Country, or a well-bred New Yorker whose patrician ways nevertheless made a bob of obeisance to the mystique of English culture – all these, however overcome by Berry's genuine and convincing enthusiasm for his wine, still had a reasonable chance of being intimidated by his fastidiousness, his insistence on the niceties of a correct attitude to a wine as good as the elixir he was offering: a perhaps irritating exactitude about its handling, decanting, temperature, the shape of the glass into which it was poured, even a censorship of the corkscrew it was proposed to use.

Such a confrontation of orthodoxy and galloping enthusiasm would normally lead to a balanced transaction, a moderate order. The case was altered, however, when Berry's customers, after long acquaintance, had accepted his meticulous insistences as justified rather than pernickety, and so soundly based as even to be worth imitation. With the brake not operating, and Francis discussing his wines with an informed eagerness that approached poetry, Berry could virtually sell what he liked. He discreetly accepted no praise for this, but in the United States particularly he turned the compliment on his hosts. He often said that there was never any credit in selling a good product, expecially to customers so alert as the Americans.

Francis Berry had been a constant visitor to the United States since 1909, and apart from supplying the Rockefellers of the nation he had formed a rewardingly appreciative market with the principal gentlemen's clubs. From his firm's point of view he was a particularly bright star glowing in the right place in the firmament at just the right time. Berry Brothers and Company, while enjoying the trappings of their cosy ancient image in the shadow of St James's Palace and the glamour of the Regency and Victorian aristocracy who had patronized them, had logically outgrown that frame. The British territorial and commercial empire was expanding at speed, and there were well-to-do gentlemen in Baltimore and Buenos Aires, Singapore and Shanghai, with gaps in their cellars which Berry Brothers could fill. And when Mr Francis Berry finally arrived, with his good looks and his culture, following his samples and apparatus in procession like a priest preceded by holy symbols, the Berry wine-tasting became an urbane, nostalgic and entirely memorable occasion.

It is difficult to cast such a dedicated vintner in the role of Whisky Baron.

Berry Brothers had sold whisky as long as any other traditional wine merchants which, in truth, was not long. The whisky explosion was then only a generation old. Before the Buchanans and the Dewars had set off south across the Border on their cutting-out expeditions, Berrys had sold whisky – Irish or Scotch as preferred, no distilleries, blends or brands mentioned – at thirty-six shillings a case of one dozen bottles. It was the same price as their ordinary champagne, their superior sherry and claret and their second-quality port (but 'Spanish Port, for Parish and Charitable use was only eighteen shillings a dozen). Queen Victoria had always been a whisky drinker, egged on by her 'Highland servant', the proprietary John Brown, who even put Scotch in his Sovereign's tea. King Edward VII, possibly because he loathed the guts of John Brown and had a therapeutic burst of energy in breaking up the statues of Brown immediately after his mother's death, hardly touched whisky. But the aristocracy had taken to it, and Berry Brothers produced their own blend. Whisky was still the poor relation in the St James's Street cellars, however, until Francis Berry took over full supervision of the export department. Whisky, he recognized, was not only the darling drink of the British sahib in the innumerable outposts of his far-flung empire; it was a 'natural' export. It did not need the mollycoddling due to wine in transit. It neither worked up a ferment nor threw a sediment. Ships and trains and bullock carts failed to shake it from its blended formula. Send out more Scotch.

Francis Berry's sales exertions in the United States were therefore not confined to wine. His export drive was consequently all the more affected by the onset of Prohibition there. In 1917, when the United States entered World War I, Congress enacted the prohibition of the manufacture of alcoholic drinks, theoretically to conserve food products by not allowing cereals and fruit to be diverted. It was ostensibly a wartime measure only, and it did not forbid the import of alcohol, but the writing was on the wall. By December 1917 the powerful Anti-Saloon League had forced through Congress a prohibition amendment to the Constitution declaring that the consumption of alochol should be banned from a date twelve months after three-quarters of the States had ratified the amendment. Prohibition duly became operative on 16th January 1920. From then on, it was an offence to manufacture, transport, import, export, sell or barter any beverage containing one-half per cent of alcohol – which made whisky about forty times too strong for the Constitution. The 'great experiment' was on. It was a fourteen-year exercise that resulted in total practical failure as a bid to stop the consumption of alcohol, which it advanced from a pleasant practice into an obsession. And, far more significantly, it laid the foundations of a system of lawlessness and corruption from which the States never fully extricated themselves.

Neither the 18th Amendment nor the Volstead Act defining prohibited alcohol forbade the entry into the United States of wine merchants. And Francis Berry accordingly made the voyage in 1921. One of his fellow passengers on board the liner was William Eugene (Pussyfoot) Johnson, the teetotal advocate who had done more than any other single person to push Prohibition through. He was now, at the age of sixty, committed to world-wide propaganda, although in his time he had been an efficient federal agent, enforcing the law in states, like Oklahoma, which had already passed unilateral declarations of addiction to forced teetotalism. He had secured thousands of convictions against local bootleggers – the name comes from a special leather bottle built into a riding boot by resourceful English smugglers of an earlier time – by sudden pounces, so swift and unexpected that he had truly earned the nickname Pussyfoot.

Johnson, though pompous, had no great sense of rancour when meeting an English wine merchant, which was magnanimous in view of the fact that two years earlier he had had one eye blinded at a London temperance rally when ragging

Three weeks after Prohibition became law, 33,100 gallons of wine were pumped into the gutters in Los Angeles.
Radio Times/Hulton

students kidnapped him and paraded him down the Strand. Though conceding that Francis Berry was too far pickled in the wine business to be extricated, he earnestly counselled him, for the sake of the financial return, to enter his son for the Church rather than into Berry Brothers, 'Permit me to recommend that your son be trained for the Cloth rather than the Wine Trade, which I assure you is a vanishing industry.' Berry tolerantly refrained from argument, and forbore to mention the money Pussyfoot Johnson himself was drawing from the Prohibition campaign. 'A dull dog,' he wrote him off later, 'with a big salary and a liking for big cigars.'

Francis Berry was not going to the United States to attempt to change the Prohibition laws – which were America's business –

or to contravene the regulations as they stood though, that might have been construed as his business. He did not disguise his feelings, but would not meddle in internal affairs. On an open battlefield, such as the whole of uncommitted Europe, when Pussyfoot Johnson (who was still going strong at the age of eighty) brought his propaganda machine into the campaign, Berry was uncompromisingly belligerent. He was one of the leaders of the Ligue Internationale des Adversaires de la Prohibition. But at the time when Berry found Pussyfoot Johnson a fellow traveller, he was on an open mission to sell, with the utmost legality, 'liquor' – that generic American term which he found as distasteful as the word 'rum-runner' when the principal product being wafted into America was Scotch whisky.

Berry Brothers and Company, with its enormous long-standing prestige, and its inextricable connection with the Court of St James's, could not possibly become directly involved in the illegality associated with challenging the domestic American Prohibition law. The firm could not even condone rum-running. What it could do and would do was to make a courteous reply to a British agent requesting shipments to a British colonial port, get the goods in as fast as possible, make a personal appraisal of the potential capacity of the market, ask no questions about rum-running – and do its damndest to ensure that the Berry Brothers products finally drunk by Americans were the untainted goods that had left St James's Street or the Glasgow warehouse.

Rum-running itself – consigning wines and spirits to the hold of a ship flying anything but the Stars and Stripes – was not illegal under any international law unless and until the vessel penetrated United States coastal waters; though in later years the British Government, in an excess of complaisant authoritarianism, made arrangements or adjusted blindfolds which permitted United States vessels to fire on the Red Duster many hundreds of miles out into the Atlantic.

Bootlegging – getting the goods into American territory – was an illegal enterprise best left to Americans, as was the ascending scale of violence and horror which stemmed from the handling of bootleg liquor – piracy on the high seas, to which even 'legal' rum-runners were vulnerable; hi-jacking, the robbery with violence of the goods whilst in transit on American territory; 'cutting' – the adulteration of genuine spirits with water, moonshine, or poisonous wood alcohol – which had the result that for every bottle of Scotch sent from Scotland a dozen of spurious 'Scotch' were drunk in the States, with a consequent trail of blindness, paralysis, and death; and the multiple murders that resulted from the gang warfare between the various protection organizations who had moved in on every stage of the highly profitable transfer of liquor from shipper to consumer. All this, in actuality, was what Prohibition entailed, and at no stage of the fourteen-year experiment did the evils ever lessen. Conditions consistently deteriorated.

When Francis Berry arrived in New York in 1921, the contravention of Prohibition was reaching the end of its first stage. America had not suddenly destroyed all its vast reserve of liquor stocks on the night of 16th January 1920, when the new law came into effect. The holdings were transferred into government warehouses, from which theoretically they could be withdrawn only by official permit for such uses as 'medicinal purposes'. In fact, although it was formally against the law, the government also indulged in a certain amount of trading of the liquor reserves for export purposes. The fact that liquor could be withdrawn, in intended small doses, optimistically destined for pharmacists, was the loophole through which a vast amount was in fact withdrawn – by presenting forged permits. None of the minor officials examined the forgeries too precisely, in view of the wad of sweeteners that were presented at the same time. It was the beginning of the system of graft that was to strangle the American public services.

This phase came to an end as Prohibition enforcement was stepped up by an enormous recruitment of manpower, allied with the fact that the considerable emergency stocks held for medicinal purposes were steadily petering out. (The typical black-market situation followed, in which doctors profited from the scarcity by increasing their charges for a prescription. The number of Americans with incurable conditions demanding the application of stimulants did not increase, but the price of Scotch at the druggists grew markedly higher.)

The bootleg trade summed up the situation, and concluded that, with the depletion of domestic resources, the overseas market would have to be more strongly tapped. It was a great day for Scotch. Rye and bourbon whiskies were out, or what came in was suspect.

Millions of Americans clutched at Scotch as a drowning man clasps a straw – and found that they were being sustained by the most accommodating survival-raft they had ever experienced. All would be well – as long as the supplies were available, and their integrity was assured. It was in this purposeful humanitarian spirit that Francis Berry was sailing to America.

The United States was the quickest connection for Nassau. Nassau, population 20,000, was the chief port on New Providence Island, a sausage of land only 21 miles long, and was capital of the 700 islands and 2000 rocky cays known as the Bahamas. Nassau was and is only 175 miles from Miami. (Bimini, where the capacious premises of the Bimini Rod and Gun Club were constantly stocked with liquor from the Nassau warehouses, was less than half that distance, and Settlement Point in the group of the Grand Bahamas, also victualled by Nassau, was 65 miles from Jupiter Inlet, near Palm Beach, Florida.)

Most important of all, Nassau was British.

Nassau had a long history of rough-and-tumble sea adventure. Columbus made his first transatlantic landfall near by. The Spanish evicted its British population several times, and when the British came back they made it a pirate haven. The Americans briefly took it in 1776. When the British repossessed it, they smuggled slaves into the Southern states from there. In the American Civil War the Nassau blockade-busters ran munitions to either side for the best price, and revitalized the prosperity of the islands. American Prohibition clearly offered the same opportunities all over again.

There was the local market of Florida and South Carolina. But of far greater potential was the stretch beginning to be called Rum Row, the lane of water extending (at a diplomatic distance out to sea) from Montauk Point, Long Island, to Atlantic City, New Jersey – a 150-mile crescent enclosing New York. It became a floating market of up to 100 ships at anchor, on the high (and sometimes very high) seas of international waters, and it was open to any shopper who could afford a motor cruiser and the not outrageous wholesale prices – and who would take his own chance of getting the loot ashore – to come alongside, compare prices, shop around and, after sampling the product, purchase a few hundred cases of liquor on offer.

Rum Row was 900 miles from Nassau, a little over three days at twelve knots, or five days at seven knots – the sort of general speeds the rum-runners maintained. According to capacity, and the state of the market and the weather and the zeal of the revenue cutters, a schooner could, in the early days, take 5,000 cases of Scotch out of Nassau, hang about selling it at a profit of only $10 a case, and be back before the month's end in plenty of time for the crew to get enduringly and paralytically drunk in Grantstown, the 'low' end of Nassau, on the $360 they had earned. For this trip the captain would have earned $1,000 (against the $75 a month which was then the going rate for a mate in the mercantile marine). The organizers would have $50,000 from which to pay the month's expenses and wages. Later, capacities increased and profits quadrupled – on paper, when they could be garnered without embezzlement or payment of protection money.

Francis Berry landed in New York, sampled what vigorous bootleg liquor was available, more in a spirit of professional research than from any devotion to nausea, chatted with old customers for old time's sake and in the hope of a better future, and took the train to Miami. There he boarded a tub called the *Mystery J*, at that time the only regular communication with the Bahamas. Outside the coastal limits the steamer passed, but did not pause at, Miami's own miniature Rum Row – knots of fairly small craft and cabin cruisers from Settlement Point with their liquor price-lists displayed on a board hanging over their side, rather like ice-cream stands.

Berry arrived in Nassau and booked in at the Lucerne Hotel. It was mainly a residential building where a number of British administrators had apartments, including Mr 'Buzfuz' Blenkinsop, the Chief Justice of the Bahamas. The proprietor was a tiny and gentle middle-aged New England lady who passed among her guests from time to time enquiring after their welfare with frail, queenly courtesy. Once settled in, Berry sallied out into Bay Street, the principal commercial thoroughfare, and located his agent.

Nassau was a white, sleepy, sun-kissed town. Bay Street itself was a pretty scruffy collection of timber-built stores, with horsecabs standing mainly idle in the shade of the women's-tongue trees. But on higher ground, above the commercial centre, there were fine white houses with shuttered windows set amid attractive gardens bright with bougainvillaea and hibiscus. You looked down across banana groves and almond trees to the silver beach, with its old Spanish fort at one end, and a coral reef beyond. The harbour front, at Rawson Square, was moderately busy with the between-trips activity of its fishing fleet, which mainly fished for sponges and turtle. The sponges lay on plucked palm leaves, drying in the sun. A small tramp was unloading supplies. Nassau had to import to live, and even brought in foreign water – people who took water with their Scotch had to buy it at three shillings and sixpence a bottle. At one active sector of the waterfront two schooners swarmed with

Negroes who were loading cases of whisky from a cluster of small carts drawn by donkeys.

Berry got down to serious business talk with his agent. Demand was high, and the prospect was that it would get much higher. It was all, of course, legitimate business. Whisky was being cleared out of bond in London or Glasgow and consigned to the British port of Nassau. Most importers could get whisky at £3 a case. An agent with an exclusive tie-up would get an appreciable discount on that. The Bahamas Government ruled that the imported spirit should be stored in government warehouses, where a duty of 24 shillings a case was imposed. Translate that into dollars, the only viable currency of the Caribbean – and there were then nearly five dollars to the pound sterling – and whisky was being brought in at $15 a case and withdrawn to the trade storehouses in Bay Street on payment of a further $6, making $21 a case. Allowing a very reasonable profit to the agent – more substantial because of the high demand, but always conditioned by the competition between him and his fellow merchants – the agent could sell the whisky to whomever he liked (which in practice meant only to a rum-runner), who would again sell it, and again in competition, in Rum Row, at a price which in the early days varied between $35 and $50 a case according to reliability and quality.

Reliability – that was Berry's main concern. He received bona fide orders and fulfilled them. From the immediate financial aspect, he had no further interest in the whisky once it had left Great Britain. The other transactions were other people's business, but they did concern him inasmuch as it was his label on the product.

'How can we stop the stuff being cut?' he asked the agent.

'We have no final control on what happens once it's in the States,' he was told. 'But even there I think it's still possible to work up respect for a name. What we can control is what the rum-runners carry. Nassau has a pretty good reputation for not tampering with the goods. There are dreadful things being done in Havana.' (Cuba is the island immediately south of the Bahamas Group, and its capital, Havana, is some 300 miles south-west of Nassau.) 'And the stuff being loaded from Havana already has a bad name. It's my belief that even the bootleggers need some quality brands, totally reliable and sworn uncut by the bootleggers themselves, if only because they must have *some* straight products for the quality trade that they can justifiably charge a very high price for.

'So anyone who is concerned with quality ought to start from Nassau. And he should get the stuff through by using the straightest man in Nassau. None of my arrangements is any business concern of yours, but perhaps you'd like, out of personal interest, to meet my friend Bill McCoy. He'll be at the Lucerne.'

The bar at the Lucerne was dominated by a very tall, very broad-shouldered, very maritime monument of a man, Captain William McCoy, who was conducting a boisterous conversation with two smaller men. McCoy was a sheer piratical character in the best boys' magazine mould. He was a pioneer rum-runner, and had often taken the goods all the way to the beach. That was in the very early days, when it had been a clean fight with the revenue men and no prospect of machine-gunner hi-jackers awaiting him on the shore – nor of the detailed demoralization of mandatory corruption and intimidation of the Prohibition-enforcement men by extensive bribes and blackmail. McCoy, who had founded Rum Row, was a highly astute sailor at sea – when it was a case of professional nautical duelling to outsail the revenue men – and a rumbustious buccaneer of a man ashore, with a loud laugh and the cheek 'of the devil'. In Nassau, until the Federal agents began to make clandestine descents with the object of kidnapping him on British territory and hustling him off to their own jurisdiction, he was fairly safe and often impudent. He had a running war with the American Consul, Loren Lathrop, who enjoyed his company and admired his guts, but reported to the United States every time McCoy left harbour. Yet, when the first touch of prosperity from the rum-running began to make its mark on Nassau, and the authorities decided they could afford to deepen the channel into the harbour – which would naturally open the port to bigger and better-paying rum-runners – McCoy went to Lathrop to propose a commercial deal that they should jointly bid for the contract, the bait for Lathrop being that they would use American dredgers. Lathrop wryly agreed. The Bahamas Government awarded them the contract. And American dredgers cleared Bahamas sludge to get more British ships running Scotch whisky to the States.

As a rum-runner, McCoy's most remarkable asset was his integrity. Like Berry, he was very sensitively concerned with the reputation of his own name. In a business deal he gave absolute honesty, and that covered the personally guaranteed quality of the product he was selling. Eventually, as Berry's agent foresaw, even the gangsters needed some criterion of reliability to give a consumer faith in some of the hooch they were selling. The practice grew up by which they used the name of the shipper, rather than the distiller or blender, as a hundred-per-cent guarantee of the integrity of the product. *This is the real McCoy* is now a by-word. In the golden years of Prohibition it was the most solemn affirmation of quality which an illegal drink-trader could make. But it was, of course, owlishly taken up by the illegal drinker.

In a harsh and powerful voice – for McCoy had been a deep-sea skipper under sail before the days of megaphones – the captain was ribbing the American Consul, using as a stick with which to beat his compatriot none other than Chief Justice Blenkinsop, the Head of the Supreme Court of the Bahamas. The drinks, as usual, were on McCoy.

'I appeal to you, Judge,' he was saying. 'I never break the law. My cargo is shipped into Nassau, and Bahamas duty is paid. I give employment here, I bring prosperity. I sell my cargo in international waters. I can't imagine what happens to it afterwards, but I am certainly no accessory to smuggling. Smuggling is the illegal import of goods into a country without payment of customs, excise or revenue duties. If my liquor ever gets inside the United States, the revenue is cheated of no money. The law of the United States says that liquor is a prohibited commodity. And since the law doesn't recognize liquor, it can't impose no duty on what it don't permit. No duty payable, no duty dodged – no smuggling. Now how about that, Loren?' And he gazed at the American Consul with open self-satisfaction.

Berry was introduced to McCoy and the others. When the talk became general, he drew McCoy aside and put a question to him.

'If you were starting from scratch,' he said, 'putting a new Scotch on the market specifically blended for American and Canadian taste – after this Prohibition nonsense is finished, of course,' he interjected swiftly, 'what would you tend to go for?'

McCoy thought for a space of time, and addressed the subject pontifically.

'Well, there's more than one whisky,' he began. 'There's no bad whisky, but there's several sorts of good. There's your rye and your bourbon, which is special and regional, there's your corn, there's your Canadian rye, there's your Scotch malt. You English have never given much credit to the rye, which is a mistake because the cereal is malted there, too. The Scotch used to make whisky from rye at one time,' he added with surprising but entirely accurate scholasticism. 'But I'll allow they used the pot still. However, you're talking about Scotch, which is malt. Or a blend of malt and corn. Now you'll agree that there are some malts which lie heavy on the stomach, which I take it is why you began blending at all. You tend to be a little religious about heaviness, in your beer as well as your whisky. If I were starting afresh, and tempting a palate which was used to the drier taste of rye ... And I take it that that's what you're concerned with?' he interjected blusteringly.

Berry made no reply.

'If I were starting afresh, I'd play down the heavy aspect of the malt. Don't diminish it, or you've lost the smooth flavour of your scotch. But you'll find softer malts to use, without using neutral spirit, which you'll no doubt declare is the sin in American rye ... '

McCoy stopped and glanced suspiciously at Berry, who was

staring at him with ironic amusement.

'Is something wrong?' said McCoy.

'Have you been reading my confidential correspondence?' asked Berry.

McCoy bristled at the reflection on his honour, then recognised the remark as Limey humour. 'Pipe down, partner,' he said, pleasantly enough.

'Tapping the cables? Burgling the board room? Suborning my secretary?'

'I don't know how to suborn, and that's a fact,' said McCoy. 'But if your secretary is as big a dude as you are, I don't mind trawling my net.'

' ... Because you and I are twin souls,' said Berry. 'Except that you are much more blunt about your home product than I should be. That's because I'm a bit of a dude.' Berry, keeping his business discretion on a tight rein, still talked long and learnedly to McCoy in the enthusiasm of meeting a man who knew his subject. 'And the colour should be true!' he ended. 'I have utter scorn for artificial colouring in either wine or spirit.'

'A light blend, a light aspect,' said McCoy. 'A whisky matured in sherry casks need never be darker than pale sherry.'

'I'm exceedingly obliged to you for your remarks,' said Berry. 'I never expected to hear such depth of thought from a layman.'

'Layman!' objected the captain without a twinkle in his eye. 'You're discussing Scotch with a McCoy!'

'McCoy,' said Berry reflectively. 'Then you're an Irish layman.' And he found room in his own eye for a twinkle. He deliberately changed the subject. 'How do you think business will go in the future?' he asked.

'It will get rougher,' said McCoy. 'They have been easy days up till now. But the opposition is getting harder. The risks will be greater, which means that the profit will be higher, which means that it will pay better to use violence. Already they're forming private armies.'

He paused, then added, 'I don't sail without my own armament nowadays, you know. Already, skippers have been overpowered and shanghaied by their crew. Nobody sails with me in the mood for mutiny, but piracy isn't dead just because we've stopped wearing black patches and wooden legs. You can still be boarded on the high seas. Especially when you're lying at anchor.'

He chuckled. 'Last trip but one,' he said, 'a craft came out to meet me by arrangement. They said they could take 800 cases. The price was agreed, but they said they'd pay after I had offloaded. I said that wasn't my style, so they paid up. Then they tried to get aboard me to twist the cash back again. I had been watching them. I waited till they needed both hands to climb aboard. I had two shooters in my hands and my mate had another. 'What is it you're buying?' said I. 'Whisky, or a crown of glory?' 'Whisky,' they said, and they dropped back into their boat and made off.'

McCoy uttered a timber-shivering laugh, and turned round and slapped Lathrop cripplingly on the back. 'What are you buying?' he roared. 'Whisky, or a crown of glory?'

'Whisky,' said the consul. 'All round.'

Francis Berry passed on to further destinations. On his return to London the directors of Berry Brothers resumed their interrupted and now prolonged discussions on the introduction of a new blend of whisky for the export market, paying full regard to the long-reiterated insistence of Francis Berry on the necessity for a light, true-coloured Scotch.

This was the conception and gestation of Cutty Sark, a new blend of malt and grain finally approved in 1923, and for many years not offered to the home market. The name was the suggestion of the Scottish artist James McBey, who had been engaged to design a distinctive label and energetically advocated the unorthodox brand name. The classically fine-lined clipper *Cutty Sark*, for long the fastest ship afloat, had recently had a rebirth into public esteem when she was bought and restored by Captain W H Dowman, a British master mariner who had once, as an apprentice, seen the clipper outrace his steamship. But the image of this lithe vessel, with at one time six spreads of sail on her mainmast alone, inevitably recalled – and perhaps not out of sheer coincidence on the part of Berry Brothers – the agile Atlantic schooners which were still the main fleet of the rum-runners of the 1920s. Diminished in size to about a quarter of the tonnage, only two-masted and not carrying full canvas – they typically carried a jib, jumbo, foresail and storm trysail and used two engines of perhaps 100 bhp each – they were not only extremely tough and reliable in withstanding the devastating Atlantic weather, but in storm conditions could sail faster than any pursuer. In one famous run a Newfoundland schooner kept up seventeen knots for twelve hours.

However, Francis Berry took passage in the more orthodox Atlantic liner on his next trip to the United States, to introduce the new Scotch whisky to his legitimate market in Nassau. He found New York far more intensely engaged with the business of acquiring and dispensing liquor, almost as a status symbol. It was like the fever of an unnecessary war, when social conversation, individual effort and disproportionate expenditure of private means had become diverted to pursuing an innocent pastime which had been hoicked up, aggrandized and elevated into a war aim.

A social glass, which in St James's implied an easing of tension, good company, and the enrichening appreciation of the handiwork of gifted men was, in uptown New York, both anti-social and unsociable – typically gulped from a hip-flask in a men's lavatory. Even in company it was taken with tension, and the reaction of the palate was discounted in favour of the effect on the gut. In a night club, where you were expected to drink, you knew that you were paying extra money in two ways – a bonus to the bootlegger for getting the drink and a bonus to the police for leaving you alone. And, even then, you could not be sure that this was not the odd night when the police made their routine raid for the entry on the record. So the general impulse was to get tanked up as fast as possible, because what was already in the liver could never be found in the flask. The graft and violence which were inseparable from this artificial decivilization were accepted as a contemporary fact of life. The most cynically offered invitation which Francis Berry received was to a party given by a middle-rank politician to celebrate his hard-won appointment to the Prohibition Enforcement Bureau. The reception in his apartment ran high with liquor that the host himself had just run in to New Jersey wearing his other hat as a bootlegger. It was amply paid for out of the first set of bribes he received for passing information on the imminent tactics of the enforcement officers.

Berry took the train to Miami, and there found that the Bahamas crossing was now so popular that a seaplane ferry service had been added to supplement the steamer. Berry still boarded the *Mystery J.* As she steamed into harbour, it was clear that Nassau had changed to a very booming port. The waterfront was jammed with schooners and steamers, while others waited their turn at anchor in the water lanes so conveniently deepened by the contract dredgers. Among them was the *Messenger of Peace*, formerly chartered by the Right Reverend the Bishop of Nassau and the Bahamas as a missionary ship to spread the Gospel to the outer islands, but now used as a rum-runner by the ex-Reverend Newman Dunn, who declared that his health, not to speak of his stipend, had increased a thousand per cent since he had abandoned the cloth for the sea.

All craft prominently flew the British Red Ensign and very large Union Jacks, correctly registered although most of them were American-owned. There was a background clatter of hammering and rivetting from the yards and new embryo dock-basins, for there was an incessant demand for ship repairs after the rumrunners had sat out the storms and surges of Rum Row. The most common order was for new anchors, since the ships were constantly dragging their anchors and having their cables sheer as they failed to ride out the gales. It was said that the sea bottom in Rum Row was carpeted with hundreds of lost anchors.

Bay Street was clearly booming. Most of the liquor stores there had been enlarged or preferably rebuilt, since their former feeble timber was not proof against the forcible entry which they now provoked. There was ten million dollars' worth of liquor stashed in Bay Street now, which justified its popular change of name to Booze Alley. In enclosed yards behind the stores, Negro men were breaking open cases of whisky with what seemed the utmost ferocity. But the bottles were merely passed to women who rearranged them from square dozens to triangular parcels of six, ranged three two one, round which they stitched covers of the coarse canvas called burlap. With triangular packing, the sharply raked schooners could stow double the supplies of liquor in their holds.

Berry's agent, who had met him on the water front, refused to allow him to stay at the Lucerne. 'You'll see why later,' he promised, and bore the Englishman off to his own villa. The road to the upper town was asphalted, which had not been so before. 'We can afford it,' said the agent.

The annual revenue of Nassau had soared tenfold since the end of the war, only five years previously. After improving the waterways and roads, installing electric power and a modern water supply, and building cold stores, the government still had a surplus of over a quarter of a million sterling. Even at the basic import price, between one and two million pounds' worth of liquor was being shipped in over a trading year, which in customs duties alone meant a revenue approaching the half-million, besides the prosperity and employment introduced by the great surge of business visitors. But the newcomers were changing the face of the once-quiet port in ways which were obvious even to the ear. Occasional fusillades of revolver shots burst up from the town as the two men sipped a drink on the agent's veranda. 'Don't worry,' he said. 'I doubt if they're killing anybody. They just get excited. It's like a frontier town now.'

The agent escorted Berry on a stroll in the town. Almost the first man they saw was walking backwards out of a barber's shop with the lather still on his face, and two gunmen urging him on from the shop. They turned him round and propelled him down the road. The agent recognized the white-faced captive and chuckled. 'He'll be bound for Market Street,' he explained. 'I thought Cleo would want to see him. She's heard that he has been spreading tales about the bad quality of her liquor, and I guessed she would want to see him pretty soon. There'll be no violence,' he assured Berry. 'She'll just give him a lashing with her tongue. Understandable, too. Cleo's liquor is absolutely straight.'

'Who is Cleo?' asked Berry.

'Cleopatra, the Queen of the Bootleggers, though she's not a bootlegger at all. An American girl, name of Grace Lythgoe. She has two very good agencies, one for rye and one for Scotch. She goes to the UK for her Scotch, and now that the American sources are dying she gets her rye from Europe, too. You'll meet her, she lives at the Lucerne. Don't fall for her, I don't want to lose my connection with you.'

They went into the bar of the Lucerne. It was a wild mêlée of noise. A furore of boasting, argument, reminiscence and menace rose from it as if it were a hive of extremely deep-throated, loudmouthed and consistently profane bees. Sea captains were shouting one another down as they capped the last speaker's tall story. Distillers' salesmen were insisting that they should buy the next round even though they had bought the last – quite unnecessarily, since none of their listeners had any intention of paying. Seedy-looking businessmen seemed engaged in interminable disputes to defend their tarnished honour. Some spree-drinkers in a corner sang unrepeatable nautical songs. The only customers who were quiet were a few sharply dressed men standing singly or in pairs and looking hard at selected members of the company as if making an in-depth analysis of their characters. Fragments of argument hit Berry's eardrums like individual bullets.

'If Saint-Pierre halves their duty they'll cut our trade to ribbons. We should complain to the government.'

'Which government?'

'The British Government, the Bahamas Government. It's unpatriotic.'

'How can Saint-Pierre be unpatriotic to the British Government when it's French. And talking of patriotism, what's your country?'

'America.'

'Then America gets the liquor cheaper.'

'Did you call me unpatriotic?'

'No.'

'Did you call me a slob?'

'I can't remember. But if I did, I guess I was right.'

'Hit me again.'

'Delighted.' And the petitioner was felled by a blow from a blackjack – delivered, with swift presence of mind, on his right collar bone instead of his head, as he was feeling for a gun in his waistband at the time.

'An academic argument,' observed Berry's agent, who seemed to have grown remarkably blasé since their last meeting. 'What's a difference of three dollars a case duty, when the price of protection get the goods ashore is going up by a steady two dollars every month? They really have no head for figures. In any case, who's going to bother with the Canucks in winter?'

The 'academic' argument was concerned with the lucrative role being played in the rum-running business by Saint-Pierre et Miquelon, the tiny morsel of French territory – two islands and 4000 inhabitants fifteen miles off Newfoundland – which, almost in a fit of absence of mind, had become a big whisky centre. Although, as might be expected, no French territory could be smirched with the suspicion of countenancing Prohibition, tight French protectionist laws forbade the export of any liquor which had not previously been imported from France. While the administration toiled to attend to this defect, a complicated minuet had to be arranged whereby whisky was sent to Halifax, Nova Scotia – which was officially 'dry' but would accept liquor in bond – and through this pipeline ships in Saint-Pierre were provisioned for active service in Rum Row. The arrangement resulted in a bountiful improvement in the prosperity of both Halifax and Saint-Pierre, but the fog and ice of winter made it an inadequate operation until the big steamers capable of ice-breaking began to be used. Nassau's winter temperature of 70°F always kept it a popular port for the schooners. Saint-Pierre's reduction of its customs tariff did, however, make a significant difference to her trade. The margin counted, particularly in large steamer shipments of up to 20,000 cases.

The uproar continued unabated in the bar of the Lucerne.

'We came alongside and went aboard,' one of the sea captains was declaiming. 'She was like another *Marie Celeste*. The hold was looted. There wasn't a case of liquor aboard, and not a sign of the crew. Just spent cartridge shells all over the deck.'

'The first time I was hired to take a steamer to Rum Row,' said another, anxious to cap the story, 'I don't know how many weeks I stayed there on station. When I'd discharged all my cargo I was ordered to take over the last of the cargo of a schooner that was wanted back in port – 2,000 cases of rye. Every month my principals would send out a duplicate pay-slip showing that my salary had been deposited in the bank. When I finally got ashore I found that all the pay-slips were forgeries. I didn't draw a cent. You can't trust nobody.'

'They once kept me out there so long we were starving,' said another. 'On the way south I had to ration water to one cup a day. I anchored off Mosquito Point and hailed a steamer, and traded a case of Scotch for a cask of water and fifty pounds of rice. Then that ran out. I spoke to another steamer and the captain gave me bread and water and a few cans of food. The skipper was a hard New Englander and he said "I don't want your whisky." But his chief engineer was making a high-sign from the stern. As soon as the captain had gone back into the deck-house the engineer threw a heaving line and he had hauled in a case of Scotch before the skipper could get his pipe lit.'

Captain Bill McCoy joined Berry and his agent. 'You'll notice the change in the Lucerne,' he said. 'All the respectable people have moved out, except for Chief Justice Blenkinsop, he still keeps his apartment. What a mob, eh? There are some good sailors here, though. But it's true you can't trust a soul. Cash first all the time now. You'll know I'm running quite a fleet at the moment. I left one of my schooner captains with a full cargo in Saint-Pierre while I went to Nova Scotia to meet some customers who had got word to me that they were in the market. I told my captain: "Don't open a hatch or leave this harbour until I get back." Lucky I did. When I got to Sydney, Nova Scotia, there was nobody to meet me. But a cable came to my captain with my signature on it. It said I had sold the whole cargo and he was to provision and sail to a point south-east of Scatari Island, Cape Breton, and that's a godforsaken stretch I can tell you. He was to deliver the cargo to the master of a ship who would be holding the duplicate of this telegram. Then sail to meet me in Nassau. Fortunately he remembered my orders and took not a blind bit of notice. It was all a fake. The whole operation was set up to decoy me and take over my cargo for nothing.'

McCoy surveyed the heaving bar-room, and it was clear from the reaction of anyone who caught his eye that he still dominated the place with his authority. He was the squarest crook in sight.

'They haven't had it all their own way,' he chuckled. 'The Bahamians aren't so dumb. They can tell a shellback from a horse-marine. They've sold these hoodlums some tubs in their time. Two hours out to sea in a fresh gale and the seams have opened. An acquaintance of mine, master of an oil tanker, came across a crew of them not so long ago in a schooner that should never have been trusted on a park pond. They were helpless in the storm cockpit, thigh-deep in a blend of Scotch and seawater. He discharged oil to windward and came alongside and took them off. They were too weak to tie a half-hitch and too ignorant to know what it was. He got them aboard. "A nice bunch of rats!" he told them. "I save your bloody lives, and you don't even bring a bottle aboard for me!" '

McCoy's great laugh boomed out, and even the beady-eyed mobster bosses stopped analysing the market and smiled socially towards him. The Lucerne had certainly changed, as all Nassau was changing. The unfortunate congregation of a church next to the hotel were in perpetual dismay from being unable to hear the sermon because of the bawdy songs from the bar.

They got a politely gentle hearing, but little practical support, from the owner of the Lucerne. She had demonstrated the greatest change of all. This diminutive, mild old lady had taken the Bowery to her heart. Her customers might seem a harum-scarum lot, in her opinion, but it was just their high spirits coming out. They might raise the roof occasionally, but at heart they were very nice boys. And because she treated them as nice boys, who only occasionally needed to be checked when they were naughty, they responded to her with warm affection and tried very hard to behave as long as she was looking. They bobbed their heads and said, 'Yes, Mother, I'm very sorry, Mother, I'll try not to do it again, Mother,' and waited until she had gone before they would even raise a swearword.

There was a certain innocent ignorance about it all, but perhaps a rather roguish enjoyment, as she sat upstairs in her own rooms – she was never seen in the bar except to quell a riot – and shook her head ruefully over her wild boys below. How near she came to a realization of the depths of their wildness is a lost secret now. These men were ruthless gangsters in the States, and though they had not come to Nassau to make trouble, but to make money, they had no intention of knuckling under to rivals in their own rackets. So Mother would reprimand a man for belching in the hall-lobby when he had just come in from sinking a corpse beyond the harbour reef with an anchor lashed to its feet. 'I'm sorry, Mother,' he would say with all the sincerity in the world, 'I'll really try to remember not to do it again.'

If she was deliberately near-sighted in her judgements, she must have been constitutionally and irreparably hard of hearing, or else just a crafty old puss. She could be excused if she did not recognize the words of the songs which so irked the church-goers next door, but she could hardly have defended them against the protesting congregation. Though it was true that the Devil had all the best tunes, and a large part of the bar-room bawdy was rendered in the harmony of impeccable gospel chants, it was difficult to maintain for very long that she thought they were hymns, in face of denials from those converted sinners who had experience of the words from both sides of the fence. Did her late flowering nourish innocence ... or wish-fulfilment ... or nostalgia? She is gone, with her secret smile, and has taken her enigma with her.

Bill McCoy suggested a quieter drink in his room upstairs, and as they moved up they met Grace Lythgoe, going to her own room. Berry was introduced. She seemed no pistol-packing momma at all, but what might be described, in the contemporary post-war slang, as Refined Young Lady, American Mark Two – which would make her cooler and more competent, and with a better grasp of business, than her opposite number in England. She accepted McCoy's offer of a drink. She did not in any case use the bar-room. This afforded her no more than minimal protection. An intelligent woman in the front line of the frontier outpost which Nassau had become knew well the way of the world and if she intended to continue the course she had set herself, maintained her integrity more by her own continual wit and intuition than by reliance on the retriever which always followed at her heels.

'I hear you're promoting a new blend,' she told Berry.

He looked unfazed, but quizzical. 'I suppose it's no particular secret,' he said.

'You English! You come here to sell something, and you talk about secrets! The mobsters are always the first to know, anyway.

She gave Berry her card, showing an office at 9 Market Street, Nassau, and the two whiskies for which she had agencies. He was impressed by the brands.

'What did you do with that poor unshaven rogue?' asked the agent. 'Pepper him?'

She laughed. 'I've never holed a man in cold blood. Though I don't shoot so badly, eh Bill?' McCoy confirmed that she didn't shoot so bad at all. She was one of the few agents who had ever gone on the actual rum-running operation, for purposes of her own, and they had had some firearms practice on the trip.

'I'm just back from England,' she told Francis Berry. 'I'm still pursuing my great idea, which I'm sure you've heard about. I want to cut out Nassau. Poor old Nassau, she's lovely, but she's costly.

'Balderdash,' said Berry's agent. 'It costs you practically nothing to live here, and there's nothing else to spend your money on, anyway. If it's twelve shillings rebate a case that's troubling you ...

'Nassau is costly because it almost doubles the distance to

Rum Row. Because the liquor has to be handled four times when it need only be handled twice – and the stevedores may be cheap here, but the breakages are not. Because Nassau is taking six dollars on every case towards servicing my damn telephone, which has been on the blink for the last three days. I don't want to cut out Nassau and take on Saint-Pierre. I want to by-pass Nassau, run a direct service from England, charter a really big ship and have it as a permanent store in Rum Row – a huge floating emporium, undercutting anybody else because its stock costs less. Keep it stocked up with supply vessels from Glasgow ...'

'Then you've got your four handlings a case back on the schedule,' said Berry's agent.

'What about the diplomatic reaction?' asked Berry. 'Keeping a huge ship at permanent moorings has got to have tacit government approval. Who's going to offend whom? And who first?'

'Where are you going to recruit your crew?' added McCoy. 'It takes real sailors to tackle all the emergencies of a rum-running trip. You won't get *them* from chippies and painters on the *Mauretania*.'

'*Men!*' shouted Grace Lythgoe with something approaching McCoy intensity. 'You don't want modern ways. You want to go on playing pirates. I tell you, if only I had a few more hard-headed women around me, I'd get this operation set up in no time at all.' There was a knock on the door, and a man slid in without waiting for an invitation.

'Hello, Mike,' said McCoy, and was about to introduce the visitor to Berry when he stopped.

Taken into custody. Twelve hundred cases of Scotch being unloaded from the British schooner *America* captured with a crew of five off Montauk Point, Long Island, New York. *Radio Times/Hulton*

'Are you in trouble?' he asked.

'Well, worried,' said Mike.

'Then take your hand off that gun, because it worries me much more.' McCoy walked to the man with his hand outstretched and was given the .38 revolver which Mike had been tensely clutching on his hip. 'What's the trouble?'

'I sold a load of liquor to Frankie and Maurice. I didn't taste it, but I knew the source and I thought it was straight. I've heard since that it was bad liquor. They say Frank and Maurice are back in town gunning for me. They've stoked up with a two-hour session in the bar-room of the Allan Hotel. Maurice is terrible when he's angry. They say he is very angry now.'

'Let's go along to your room,' suggested McCoy. 'Better leave your thirty-eight behind at the moment.' He slung the gun in a drawer and motioned to the others to stay in his room.

At that moment the door of McCoy's room was kicked open. A very large man stood there, rather smartly dressed for Nassau, with a shiningly shaved but nevertheless gaboon-blue jowl rising like a sombre full moon from the collar of his immaculate white shirt. He seemed in a dangerously quiet stage of drunkenness. In each hand he held a revolver. As he stood in the doorway a figure passed down the corridor. The man called over his shoulder, 'Hey, Judge, can I have your attention for a second?'

Waving his right-hand revolver, he made way for Chief Justice Blenkinsop to come into the room.

'Judge, I'd like you to take a look at that man there. The one with the bulbous eyes and the white face. There is also a yellow belly and a lily liver, but these will not be visible until the postmortem examination is concluded. If ever that man comes before you as a two-timer, double-crosser and general knife, I advise you, order new cordage for your cat-o'-nine-tails. But that situation is very unlikely, because the defendant Mike Callaghan and myself are just about to duel to the death with these pistols I have so thoughtfully provided.'

Angry Maurice casually fired from his right hand a shot which buried itself in the timber floor about an inch in front of Mike Callaghan's left toe. He then twirled both guns into the air, caught them by the barrels, and pushed them forward towards Callaghan with the invitation, 'Pistols for two.'

'Oh, pardon me,' he interjected. 'Fair's fair.' And he span the guns again, caught them by the grips, and fired from his left hand a bullet which made the same accurate marking near Callaghan's right toe. He twirled his armament again and shoved them forward.

'Well, thanks very much,' said Chief Justice Blenkinsop, with easy English urbanity. 'I'll remember what you say. You'll realize, of course, that as Chief Justice I don't deal with petty crime or even felony, unless the case comes for appeal. In the meantime, I congratulate you on your marksmanship – but do keep missing, won't you?'

And with a courteous smile he retired to his apartment.

'This is my room you're splintering,' said Bill McCoy, 'and there is a lady present. You can thank your lucky stars that Mother is away for the day. Maurice, Mike, shall we go along to Mike's room and iron this thing out?' His unforced leadership packaged up the situation. Maurice turned and went out. McCoy followed, not even looking back to cheek on Mike, who brought up the end of the file.

The agent shut the door of McCoy's room.

'Well, that's all right now,' he said.

There was a solitary shot from somewhere near by, and the sound of shattering glass. Francis Berry waited in some suspense for the sequel. It came as a high scream, which steadily grew lower in pitch until it could be recognized as helpless laughter. Then the voice of Angry Maurice could be heard through the whole hotel, which had lapsed into reverent silence following the first shot, 'You miserable punk! You shivering twicer! You are sober, and all you can hit is your own filthy liquor samples. I'm drunk and I'm going to make you dance, Callaghan, dance, dance, dance, dance, dance.' And five pistol shots punctuated the end of the harangue.

There was a hubbub of fading voices, and the door opened. Chief Justice Blenkinsop came into the room.

'They've all gone downstairs for a drink to say bygones are bygones,' he announced, and came towards Francis. 'It is Mr Berry, isn't it? Now tell me something about this Cutty Sark.'

That night the habitués of the Lucerne, exhilarated by the events of the day and assured that Mother would not return until the next morning, decided to hold a fire dance amid the palms of the hotel yard. Normally this sporadic festivity, which was an extremely uninhibited cross between old African voodoo and new Caribbean rum, was reserved for a site in a forest clearing well away from the port, beyond Grantstown, and the local police discreetly plugged their ears from the throbbing drums and orgiastic screams which trumpeted the celebration for miles around. This time the organizers brashly calculated that no police would take up the challenge even in the centre of the town. In this respect they were right, but their intelligence reports on Mother's movements were mistaken. At the height of the party, as twenty nude girls danced round the fire in the Lucerne yard and fifty drunken roughnecks bayed to the beat of the drums, a tiny woman in a straight dress and a fruit-trimmed hat pushed her way through the outer ring and stood in the firelight glaring at the whirling carousel of bobbing Negro breasts. It was Mother.

The drums stopped. The girls fled. The men stood like sheep to take their punishment. 'Boys!' said Mother in gentle reprimand. 'This is not the way to behave yourselves. Not at all. I thought better of you than this. Would you like your mothers to see you as I see you now? Put that fire out at once and go straight up to bed, everyone of you.'

And, amid shambling murmurs of 'Sorry, Mother!' and 'We didn't mean it, Mother,' the fire dance fizzled out.

Francis Berry speedily completed his arrangements in Nassau, and prepared to leave for home. He had to take a sea passage to Miami in the *Mystery J.* because a hoodlum with a grievance had blackjacked the pilot of the seaplane, who was now in hospital with a broken skull. It was a sheer mistake, as the attacker apologetically explained afterwards, done in the dark in the belief that the pilot was another hood who had double-crossed him.

Meanwhile Cutty Sark was securely launched. Its development had to be left for the moment in the experienced hands of the trade and the palates of the more sophisticated consumers, with every possible precaution taken that the customers were getting 'the real McCoy'. Necessarily therefore a fair interval of time had to be allowed before valid reactions came through. It was no simple task to create a new Scotch in these circumstances. Francis Berry, with his characteristic self-effacing joviality, admitted to no tension during the long interval of probation and claimed no laurels when it became gradually clear that they had scored a hit. And yet he above all in the company, with his hypersensitive perfectionism, would have suffered the death of a thousand cuts and would have been unable to conceal his agony, if the project had gone seriously wrong. Cutty Sark was not created for the illegal United States market. There were many other outlets, notably the important and affluent whisky-drinking aristocracy of the South American republics and the less courtly but much thirstier oil- and construction-engineers who were then developing Mexico. These were customers in whom the taste for a Scotch that was lighter but not thinner developed as soon as it was encouraged. But Berry Brothers were not so hypocritical as to pretend that the United States market was not important. And to achieve a blend which, having first satisfied the Berry experts, had next to be approved by people who were not supposed to be drinking it, was an operation with many of the subtleties of a wartime Special Operations Executive keeping in touch with pockets of the Resistance in enemy country.

It was some years before Francis Berry visited Nassau again. By this time he was an outstanding leader of the International League opposing Prohibition. Prohibition in the United States was thrashing in its vigorous and very ugly death throes. When Berry went across, Rum Row was a decayed market lane. The Prohibition Enforcement Bureau had enlisted the United States

Navy to link with the Revenue in a five-fold defence ring around New York, beginning 100 miles out with patrols of the obsolete 1918 destroyers which Roosevelt was later to put at Churchill's service in World War II. The liquor was still getting through, but in revolutionary sophistication. Big steamers were used, massive enough to resist the piratical high-seas hijacking which had become common as gangland extended its resources. They sailed under sealed orders which, when opened in a remote area of the ocean, dictated a course to be set for an even more remote stretch. Cargoes and deliveries were fully negotiated in advance in business boardrooms, and prepaid under escrow, with the cash held by a third party until signals of delivery and acceptance had been received. No cash passed at sea, and no fraternization was permitted between the crews of ships which met, for fear of conspiracy and piracy. The final cloak-and-dagger detail of the transfer was when the two vessels sighted each other. Each ship's master held ten bank-notes, stacked in a certain order and all individually torn in half. The masters would speak to each other by signal, 'What is the number of your eighth note?' If the numbers coincided, the ships approached, but before actual delivery was made the halves of the torn note had to be produced to show that they married.

All these precautions, however, did not imply that gangster rule of the Prohibition contravention process was being evaded. Control had merely shifted to higher echelons of power, which demanded larger and larger armies of mobsters, wider and wider areas of corruption. The 'drys' in the United States were no longer led by the Bible-thumping Baptists from the corn-belt. The people in America who opposed the repeal of Prohibition with the greatest virulence were the bent politicians, the crooked police, the manufacturers of substitute hooch, the bottle-fakers and label-printers, and the huge criminal brigades of the bootleggers, hi-jackers, pirates, protection racketeers and pinhead gunmen. These were the operators who were making more millions from the illegal sale of liquor than the United States treasury had ever renounced when the ban was introduced, and only at the trifling cost of murdering an average of twenty people a night.

Whilst Berry was in New York, his unwelcome visitor in St James's, Mr Jack 'Legs' Diamond, was enjoying a weekend in the Monticello Hotel in that city with his mistress, the showgirl Marion Roberts, when intruders burst open the door of the room and shot him in the bed. He did not die. He had survived many assassination attempts before. In hospital he asked to be placed in the bed of honour where the gangster chief Arnold Rothstein had died – Diamond had been his principal bodyguard on that occasion and had stopped the first bullet. From his hospital bed he declared, with a weak grin, 'I ain't got the slightest idea why I was shot. I'm just a young fellow trying to get ahead.' What he omitted to say was that, after having been arrested on five different occasions for homicide (and on sixteen other occasions for other felonies) he had so contrived matters that he had never taken the rap for any crime since his desertion from the army, and rival gangland execution squads were trying to do what the police had so far signally failed to achieve for this young fellow trying to get ahead.

Diamond's occupation was beer-runner, racketeer and protection extortioner. Recently, to remind the night-club world that non-payment of protection money had serious disadvantages, he had shot the two owners of the Hotsy-Totsy Club dead in the middle of their own dance-floor at the height of the evening's entertainment. He still got away with it. His accomplice was put on trial eventually, but Diamond saw to it that everyone who was prepared to testify at the trial was murdered beforehand. The accomplice was acquitted for lack of evidence. Diamond then surrendered to the police who were officially seeking him, and since there was no one left to identify him as the murderer, he was freed. At this point the gangster Dutch Schulz decided that Diamond should be cut out of the New York City liquor racket, and he was powerful enough to do it. Diamond retreated to up-state New York, where he took over the beer interests. But Schulz still pursued him. Diamond demonstrated his authority with local roadhouse speakeasies by shooting one owner in order to encourage the others. But matters became too hot and he had to leave the States temporarily. He was ignominiously refused entry into Great Britain and France, and thrown out of Germany, from where he was deported in a tramp steamer. He was formally re-arrested on arrival in the United States, but was naturally released, and his botched execution in the Hotel Monticello followed. He then became engaged in torture, rather than murder, to maintain his shaky beer empire. This was a mistaken decision, since it left live victims who would talk, rather than dead men who could not. A police chief was found with guts enough to prosecute him and he was put on trial. He emerged on $25,000 bail and was sprayed with sub-machine gun bullets as he came out of the courthouse. After an eight months' delay he was finally acquitted. It was by this time his twenty-third acquittal on charges ranging from murder through robbery with violence to trafficking in drugs and prostitution. On the night of his acquittal Diamond celebrated with his mistress in a wild carouse at an Albany night club. He went away alone to sleep it off in a boarding house where he was holding a room under the name of John Kelly. Just before dawn, as he was preparing for bed, he was shot dead in his silk underwear. In twelve years of major crime he had been found guilty of one offence only – he was ordered to pay a nominal fine for violating the Federal Prohibition law. It was a period when justice, if not blind, did tend to squint. Even Diamond's own underworld was more just to him. It rubbed him out.

Diamond died as Prohibition, which he and his associates had striven so hard to preserve, was on its death-bed, too. The good sense and civic judgement – and, in the end, the skilful argument – of people like Francis Berry, men of culture even if they were reprehensible wine-bibbers, were justified in the end. But Francis had retired from Berry Brothers before the formal appeal of the 18th Amendment. This did not mean that he failed to keep an eye, from his very active retirement, on the progress of Cutty Sark. His rivals joked that this remarkable blend of Scotch was the whisky of immaculate conception – a potion accurately prepared according to the abstract formula of partners who were mainly known as connoisseurs of fine wine. Francis merely smiled acknowledgement, and watched the blend steadily climb in popularity among the newly legalized drinkers within United States. When World War II broke out, Francis had bequeathed to the nation the whisky whose export earned millions of dollars for the war effort, and two fighting sons, of whom the elder, George, was killed in North Africa and the younger, Anthony, survived to become the chairman of Berry Brothers and Rudd, which was the new style of the company. In 1961 John Rudd, son of Hugh Rudd who died in 1949, and Anthony Berry could announce that Cutty Sark was the brand leader in the United States among all Scotch whiskies, and since then it has steadily increased its international sales besides biting deeper into the home market.

There were congratulations all round. But nobody took any advertising space to proclaim the insight, foresight and enterprise, thirty and forty years previously in the frontier town of Nassau, of Francis Berry, the most fastidious and least flamboyant Whisky Baron of all. A generation previously, McCoy had been offering his tougher customers the belligerent alternative of whisky or a crown of glory. It seemed that Francis Berry, with judgement and patience, had achieved both.

DAICHES, DAVID, *Scotch Whisky: Its Past and Present.* London, 1969; Edinburgh, 1995

DEWAR, TR, *A Ramble Round the Globe.* London, 1904.

GUNN, NEIL M., *Whisky and Scotland.* London, 1985.

KROLL, HARRY H., *Bluegrass, Belles and Bourbon.* New York, 1967.

LAVER, JAMES, *The House of Haig.* Markinch, 1958.

LOCKHART, SIR ROBERT BRUCE, *Scotch: The Whisky of Scotland in Fact and Story.* London, 1951, 1959; Glasgow 1995

MACDONALD, JOHN, *Secrets of the Great Whiskey Ring.* New York, 1880, 1968.

MCDOWALL, RJS, *The Whiskies of Scotland.* London, 1967.

WILSON, ROSS, *Scotch Made Easy.* London, 1959. *The House of Sanderson.* Edinburgh, 1963. *Scotch: The Formative Years.* London, 1970.